The FREE FRENCH
SECRET AGENTS
The Bureau Central de Renseignements et d'Action
1940-1944

Pascal LE PAUTREMAT

with the collaboration of Jean-Louis PERQUIN and Éric MICHELETTI

This book is dedicated to the men and women whose roles and names have often been forgotten by official History or hidden for some untold reason. Nevertheless, they were genuine patriots…

They were driven by humility, dedicated to a noble cause and many died in action, in hiding or in exile. Lest we forget …

Histoire & Collections

CONTENTS

Free French para wings.

Cover.
On 14 June 1944, in the courtyard of the French Embassy in London, three BCRA agents receive the Croix de la Libération, Free France's most prestigious decoration. "Mary" Basset DSO, MC and André Jarrot DCM, MM were saboteurs during the Armada mission and Michel Pichard MBE was national coordinator for the BOA.
(ECPAD picture)

Cover.
The Forces Françaises Libres (FFL or Free French Forces) insignia. The first FFL volunteers wore a "France" woven title on their sleeves similar to those worn by Commonwealth forces. In December 1940, Caporal Louvier drew this badge which was soon nicknamed "The mosquito". The sword is surrounded by the wings of victory, a laurel wreath, the French tricolours and the "France Libre" title. The cross of Lorraine rapidly became the symbol of Free France and then of the French Résistance.

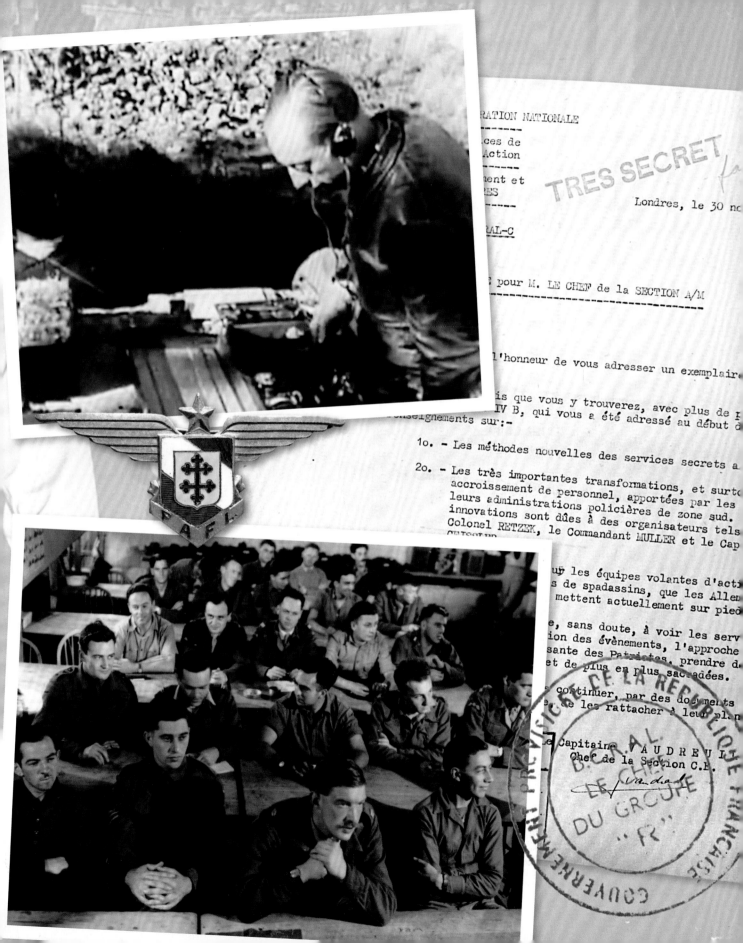

TRES SECRET

Londres, le 30 no...

... pour M. LE CHEF de la SECTION A/M

...l'honneur de vous adresser un exemplair...

...is que vous y trouverez, avec plus de p...
...IV B, qui vous a été adressé au début d...
...nseignements sur:-

1o. - Les méthodes nouvelles des services secrets a...

2o. - Les très importantes transformations, et surto...
accroissement de personnel, apportées par les ...
leurs administrations policières de zone sud. ...
innovations sont dûes à des organisateurs tels...
Colonel RETZEK, le Commandant MULLER et le Cap...
...ISSLER.

...r les équipes volantes d'acti...
...s de spadassins, que les Allem...
...mettent actuellement sur pied...

...e, sans doute, à voir les serv...
...ion des évènements, l'approche ...
...sante des Patriotes. prendre d...
...et de plus en plus sacradées.

...continuer, par des docu...ents...
...de les rattacher à leur plan...

Le Capitaine ... AUDREUIL...
Chef de la Section C.B...

The staff of the Forces Françaises de l'Intérieur (FFI or French Forces of the Interior) during the Spring of 1944. Left to right, Major Bernard Dupérier DSO, DFC, OC Ile-de-France fighter Squadron, Colonel Pierre de Chevigné, chief of staff of General Koenig, Rear Admiral Pierre Lucas, General Pierre Koenig, Colonel Passy DSO, MC, head of the BCRA and Commander Roger Raulin, Adjudant. In March 1944, General Koenig was appointed Delegate of the French Republic Provisional Governement (gouvernement provisoire de la république française or GPRF) to General Eisenhower, supreme commander of Allied forces. Koening was also the commander of French forces in the United Kingdom and commander of the French Forces of the Interior (EMFFI).
(National Archives picture)

INTRODUCTION

IN SPITE OF THE GERMAN occupation of France and unsecure lines of communications, the Resistance was able to organize itself and start a genuine counter-attack in order to ensure the political influence of the Fighting French, a Free France represented - even monopolized through a strategy of influence - by General Charles de Gaulle. This influence was nevertheless always threatened by infighting and betrayal. Charles de Gaulle was a man with a strong character and as such he left nobody indifferent; he managed to gather many around him, but still, many did not see him as the chief of a new republican regime in France... This France, which was not the one which had collaborated with nazi Germany, was not, until 1944, synonymous with Gaullism. This historical reality has often been minimized if not hidden.

Since 1944-1945, the official history has erased some of these peculiarities to the point that today the dominating picture is a Free France gathered around the person of Charles de Gaulle... Anyway, de Gaulle managed to prevail and he finally was acknowledged by the Allies as the only representative of Free France. This, in a very simplistic way, is the vision we can have of the years comprised between 1940 and 1944.

However, this does not diminish the efforts and sacrifices made by covert agents, men and women, sacrifices that have strengthened the Intelligence Gathering and Direct Action branches of General de Gaulle' secret services.

When Charles de Gaulle reached London in order to organize what was to be known as Free France, he was in search of credibility and recognition and it became crucial for him to quickly organize an intelligence and covert actions service, capable of having both a clear and an evolutionary view of the situation which was then prevailing in occupied France. This is how the Central Office for Intelligence Gathering and Direct Action (commonly referred as BCRA) was born. The task of that service was to gather military, but also political, economic and social intelligence. Its tasks also included the collection of intelligence on individuals. It also had to organize armed resistance in

occupied French territory and prepare for a new administrative organization of France in the perspective of the future liberation of the country.

Few studies have been carried out in depth on the evolution and growth of the Free French secret services from both London and Algiers and on their relationships with the networks of internal resistance movements in France. Nevertheless, sufficient information has reached us to be able to now tell the story of the volunteers and experts who, often at the cost of their lives, have given it all in the name of patriotism, because they refused to accept the victory of the enemy or just because they wanted a new France to appear from the rubbles of defeat. Of this global refusal to admit foreign domination were born numerous covert operations.

After the Second World War, and during the following decades, many surviving agents could have spoken, giving details on what they had really done, on the real dimension of inter service rivalry between the BCRA, the American secrets services of the Office of Strategic Services (OSS), the British Intelligence Service (IS) and the Special Operations Executive (SOE) or they could have told about the rivalry between Giraudists and Gaullists, a rivalry which led to severe craks characterized by pettiness or unhealthy ambitions that all ended up corrupting the collective effort.

Most of the protagonists are now dead, having remained silent throughout their lives, a silence which was only marginaly broken by a few publications. Because of their culture, mindset, and education, these actors and witnesses of the past preferred to remain in the shadows they all knew so well after having hidden in them during the dark years. Until they fought their final battle, they remained true to the intelligence community motto coined by Captain André Dewavrin DSO, MC, the man who had been entrusted by de Gaulle with the creation of the Free French secret services: "To serve and be silent".

But, in retrospect, this fact greatly complicates the historians' task who must also serve as a conduit for the dissemination and popularization of these complex, difficult or technical parts of the history of men at war, a story that has not yet finished being written, between oral history and researches in the archives[1].

This being said, let's now focus our attention on the history of General de Gaulle's secret services; their value and role cannot be overstated as well as the role they had played in the final victory of the Allies.

For clarity's sake, the name BCRA, which was effective as of September 1942 after a series of administrative reforms that will be detailed in the forthcoming pages, will be used throughout this book.

---

1. Sebastien Albertelli contributed to highlight this history thanks to his doctoral work. Cf Sébastien Albertelli. Les Services secrets du General de Gaulle. Le BCRA 1940-1944. Paris, éditions Perrin, 2010, 617 pages.

Previous page, bottom left.
André Dewawrin DSO, MC a.k.a Passy believed the French secret services had to be totally independent from the Allies in order to advocate the results of the French underground at the highest level. Interestingly, on this picture and in contradiction to his own orders, Passy wears both the Free French and the British parachute wings.
(François de Rochenoire collection picture)

Bottom.
In Septembre 1941, 186 men under the command of Major Pierre Billotte joined the Free French. They were former French POWs who had escaped German camps before reaching the USSR. They were thus known as "the Russians"; subsequently, several would serve in the ranks of the BCRA.
(ECPAD picture)

THE BCRA: AN OVERVIEW

A Free France concerned by its operational credibility

Top.
For the duration of the war, and even though he himself had served as an intelligence officer in the Lebanon during the period 1929-1931, General de Gaulle always kept a certain level of suspicion against the BCRA.
(Fondation de la France Libre picture)

IT QUICKLY became vital for General Charles de Gaulle and his close subordinates to integrate into their military staff a service dedicated to the liaison between the special services and the internal resistance movements operating on French territory. This requirement also answered Churchill's government expectations; the British Prime Minister had asked de Gaulle to create an intelligence service which could inform British services on the evolution of the situation in occupied France. Specifically, the aim was to get accurate Intelligence on German military potential, on the human and material resources of Third Reich troops, as well as a good knowledge of the network used by the Nazi administration in France. In addition, it had to collect data on operations conducted or prepared by the German forces, particularly against Great Britain. It was also essential to gather Intelligence not only on the construction of the Atlantic Wall, but also on the order of battle of the German armed forces in Normandy and in the Pas-de-Calais.

Top right.
Hand written notes sent by General de Gaulle to Major Passy in October 1941 ordering him to contact the British Secret Intelligence Service (SIS) and Special Operations Executives (SOE) in order to insure those services would not stop newly arrived Frenchmen from joining the Free French Forces.
(François de Rochenoire collection picture)

Next page.
Headquarters Free French Forces at 4, Carlton Gardens, London. The 2e Bureau (which became the BCRA in June 1942) was briefly located there in July 1940 along with the other Free French before moving to 3, Saint James Street and then finally, in March 1942 to 10, Duke Street.
(ECPAD picture)

**General de Gaulle in his Carlton
Gardens'office at the end of July 1940.**
(Fondation Charles de Gaulle picture)

To achieve this goal, the men of General de Gaulle had to establish liaison with the resistance networks.

The first step led to the creation of a "deuxième bureau" (S2, Intelligence) in General de Gaulle's headquarters, on the 1st of July 1940. This service was in charge of collecting intelligence and information of all sorts. The head of this section was Captain André Dewavrin (1911-1998) – soon to be better known under his alias of "Passy". His task was to organize this S2 section from scratch and to make sure it would soon run smoothly and efficiently for the time being. According to Dewavrin, he was given this mission in a brief meeting with de Gaulle, on the third floor of St. Stephen's House. Also present were Captain Tissier, Chief of Staff, and Lieutenant Hettier de Boislambert who had the reputation of being a skilled big game hunter; at the time, he was liaison officer to the British but he was soon to be appointed personal aide to General de Gaulle. Passy and his close collaborators had thus been approved by de Gaulle who, in those dire times, had to rely on his first impression to select men who then had to prove their worth over an extended period of time.

(continued on page 14)

Top.
Hubert Moreau was the first Free French agent deployed inside occupied France. He carried out an intelligence gathering mission.

Top.
Daniel Lomenech in British uniforme.
(Jean-Louis Le Bihon collection)

Bottom.
The Rouanez-ar-Peoc'h sailing towards Falmouth transporting Raymond Le Corre, Michel Baltas, Marcel Guénolé and Henri Le Goff while returning from Hubert Moreau's second mission inside occupied France in August 1940.
(Hubert Moreau picture)

André Dewavrin *a.k.a "Passy"*

The last boy of an industrialist family of six originating from the North of France, André Dewavrin was born on 9 June 1911. He spent most of his childhood in the 16th arrondissement of Paris and his education was strongly influenced by reliogisity. He attended the Ecole des Frères de la Doctrine Chrétienne school which was supported by General de Gaulle's father and devoted a lot of his time to the study of mathematics in two prestigious parisian schools, Saint-Stanislas and Louis-le-Grand. He then got a law degree before entering the famous Ecole polytechnique with the class of 1932-1933. In 1934, after graduating, and because the economic situation was not very bright, he choose a military career and was sent for two years to the corps of military engineers school located in Versailles. He then was posted to the 4th Combat Engineer Regiment (4th Régiment du Génie) in Grenoble. He got married to Miss Jeanne Gascheau who bore him two children, in 1936 and 1939. Between 1938 and 1939, as a Captain, he was in charge of deputy head of the fortification class at the Saint-Cyr military academy. When war broke out in September 1939, Dewavrin was in command of an Engineer company specializing in electro-mechanical support before being posted to the staff of the 9th Army located in Verviers.

In April 1940, Dewavrin took part in the Norway campaign; he was in charge of defensive works and responsible for the engineer component of the expeditionary corps. Then, he was appointed as liaison officer to the 4e Bureau (logistics) of the French staff under General Béthouart. There, he got acquainted with Lieutenant-Colonel Magrin-Vernery, of the Foreign Legion's 13e DBLE and with Lieutenant Maurice Duclos, a member of the far-right activist group known as La Cagoule (the hood) who was latter to become famous because of his extravagance but also because of his courage. After the withdrawal from Norway, on 21 June 1940, Dewavrin reached Southampton onboard the Meknès and started working for the Free French secret services. He managed to impose himself thanks to his accute intelligence and cold character but he made few friends in the process. He always kept his distances and this gave him the reputation of a cold, hard and authoritarian man. Dewavrin could have a temper and be scornful with those he had little time for; in that respect, he was not unlike his boss, General de Gaulle, in a time when one needed an extraordinary strong character to stand one's ground among the typical representatives of those times of Major crisis: gaullists and antigaullists, former members of the Vichy administration, men driven by ambition, selfish characters, traitors and opportunists but also civil servants and men ready to die for a noble cause….

In June 1943, while the special services of General de Gaulle went through an administrative merger, Passy went to Algiers to take command of the technical branch of the Direction Generale des Services Spéciaux, which was then placed under Jacques Soustelle.

In February 1944, he was appointed as Chief of Staff to General Koenig, in charge of the Free French Forces and the French Forces of the Interior. From August 1944, he took command of the FFI of the Guingamp region of Brittany and contributed, with nearly 2,500 Résistance fighters, to the liberation of the city of Paimpol.

Once France had been liberated, Dewavrin returned to the intelligence services and, between September 1944 and April 1945, carried out several missions, particularly in French Indochina. He then became head of the DGER, which soon became the SDECE. He set about to rationalize this huge structure which then had more than 10,000 people on its strength, finally retaining about 2,200. This caused the rage of many, particularly in the ranks of the Communist agents, and in response to these cuts, Dewavrin was subjected to an intense campaign of destabilization. He was accused of financial embezzlement in favour of the Gaullist party. After four months in prison and because of the lack of any tangible evidence, the charges were dropped...

In 1946, following the departure of General de Gaulle's from the presidencial office, he resigned from his official duties, and joined the world of international business.

André Dewavrin's decorations included the Distinguished Service Order, the Military Cross, the Norwegian War Cross, the Resistance Medal, the Croix de guerre 1939-1945, with four citations, and the Grand-Croix de la Légion d'honneur. He also was a Compagnon de la Libération by a May 20, 1943 decree.

Previous page, top.
On 14 June 1944, in the courtyard of the French embassy in London, Colonel Passy DSO, MC, (left) and other members of the Free French Forces' staff look on while the Cross of the Ordre de la Libération is awarded to several BCRA agents. (At this time, the BCRA had changed its name to DGSS).
(ECPAD picture)

Previous page, bottom.
An autographed picture from General de Gaulle to Colonel Passy dated 8 February 1945.
(François de Rochenoire collection picture)

Top.
As soon as the the Free French intelligence services were created Passy insisted on the 2e Bureau keeping its national identity, making sure it would not be amalgamated with the British Intelligence Service.
(Musée de l'ordre de la Libération picture)

Right.
Aged 30 in 1940, Captain Dewavrin DSO, MC, a.k.a "Passy" was an engineer instructor at the Saint-Cyr military academy. He had no previous experience in the field of covert intelligence but he managed, with very limited assets, to organize one of the most efficient secret services of the Second World War.
(Musée de l'ordre de la Libération picture)

De Gaulle also assigned Passy to command the 3rd Bureau (S3, Operations) which was tasked with the preparation and planning of operations based on intelligence obtained and processed by the 2nd Bureau. Given the magnitude of the task, Passy finally delegated the command of the 3rd Bureau to Captain Pierre de Hautecloque, a cousin of General Leclerc who was soon to make a name for himself in the deserts of North Africa. All of this happened at a time when, according to Passy, the strength of the Free French forces gathered around General de Gaulle was roughly the equivalent of a battalion.

The situation also required the development of a synergy, which required, once again, some minor adjustments. According to Passy, Hettier de Boislambert initially sent missions in occupied France unbeknownst to Passy. Passy made the point with Hettier de Boislambert and the situation changed in the following months in order to clarify the decision-making process.

Fully aware of the importance of these issues, Passy was fully dedicated to the creation of a comprehensive French secret services organization. He quickly appeared as a meticulous organizer but also as an authoritarian. While Passy was busy organizing he soon realized he would not go far without any external support; at this stage, the British were already the undisputed masters of intelligence and they could rely on solid technical and logistical support. Thus, a deal was struck between Churchill and de Gaulle on August 7, 1940 allowing the French services to receive support from the British services in their mission to identify the German capabilities on a hypothetical invasion of Great Britain. This agreement relieved the Free French of the funding issues they had been having from the start since Free France had very little financial assets when it was created in June 1940. This agreement was reinforced by a second agreement, dated March 19, 1941 by which the British government agreed to open credit lines to Free France in order to cover its military and civil expenses. However, by mid-1942, the quantity of equipment (weapons and explosives) allocated to the Free French by the SOE was still below the requested amounts.

On July 14th, 1942, Free France was renamed Fighting France and de Gaulle re-emphasized his role as a political

The Croix de la Libération being awarded to three Fighting Frenchmen in April 1943 in Camberley

Major Claude Hettier de Boislambert, Lieutenant François Martin and Michel Legrand (MC and 2 bars), both belonging to the 4e bataillon d'infanterie de l'Air (Free French 4 SAS) being awarded the croix de la Libération in April 1943 in Camberley while Colonel "Passy" looks on.

• Michel Legrand joined the Free French forces in August 1940 and was thrice wounded in action in Syria in 1941, in Libya in July 1942 and in Brittany in August 1944. He took part to Operation Franklin in 1944-45 in the Ardennes and did another combat jump over Holland on 8 April 1945 with the Free French SAS during which he saw ten days of intense combat operations against German forces.

Volunteering for a deployment to Indochina, he was wounded a fourth time in 1947. Michel Legrand then volunteered for a second tour-year tour in Indochina between December 1950 and February 1953, taking part in many other combat operations. In February 1954, he returned to Indochina a third and final time. He was part of the "colonne Crèvecœur" which tried to recover some of the escapees from the Dien-Bien-Phu siege. Michel Legrand died of exhaustion and diseases in Indochina on 29 May 1955. Married to an English woman, he also was the only French serviceman ever to receive the Military Cross with two bars.

• François Martin was a seargent posted to the mountain brigade when the Second World War broke out. He took part to the norwegian campaign of April-May 1940. Returning to the United Kingdom with the rest of the French expeditionary corps in June 1940, he opted for Free France and remained in the UK. Initially posted to the Free French Chasseurs (Light Infantry) battalion in Camberley, he was promoted to the rank of aspirant (Cornet or candidate officer) in August 1941 and sent to the Middle East. In May 1942, he joined the paratroopers of the French Squadron in Kabrit in Egypt. This unit was attached to the Special Air Service under the command of Major Stirling. Subsequently posted to the *4e Bataillon d'Infanterie de l'Air*, he was parachuted with his "stick" during the night of 9 to 10 June 1944 near Duault in the Côtes-du-Nord département. In the face of greater enemy forces, he conducted several rear-guard actions in order to protect the withdrawal of his unit to the Morbihan area. On 12 July 1944, after having been betrayed, he was shot by German forces and Vichy Milice members in the Kerihuel en Plumelec hamlet in the Morbihan département.

• Claude Hettier de Boislambert was mobilised in 1939 as a Lieutenant in a Cavalry unit. He saw action in the Somme area and in several delaying actions on the river Seine, in Normandy and in Brittany. On 16 June 1940, he escaped to the United Kingdom and offered his services to General de Gaulle who asked him to be part of his private staff. Arrested on 30 September 1940 after the failed Dakar operation, Major de Boislambert was sentenced to death by the Vichy government; the sentence was then commuted to forced labour for life. After twenty six months in jail, he managed to escape and spent another two months liaising with intelligence gathering and direct action networks. Summoned back to London by General de Gaulle, he returned to the UK during the night of 14 to 15 January 1943 thanks to a pick-up operation carried out in the Clermont-Ferrand area.

leader. The "Forces Françaises Libres" (Free French Forces - FFL) aimed at operating more closely, with the French resistance movements and networks. This could be done in a centralized or decentralized way, depending on the situation. From the end of 1943, the French resistance movements and networks were gathered into the "Forces Françaises de l'Intérieur" (French Forces of the Interior - FFI[1]). When added to the FFL, the whole constituted the "Forces Françaises Combattantes" (FFC or Combating French Forces).

THE RISE OF THE BCRA

The "Forces Françaises Libres" were built on what units were left of the French expeditionary corps after the Norway campaign of April-June 1940. Passy was among the veterans of those battles. While many decided to join North Africa, some preferred to stay in England. Volunteers were gathered in Trentham Park in the Manchester area.

The establishment of the BCRA is dated between July 1940 and August 1941. The amateurism of the very first volunteers was mitigated by their unfailing

determination. They showed a very high degree of motivation and they just wanted to be part of the adventure led by Passy. As it was obvious that Passy could not do everything alone, he had to surround himself with competent and charismatic men capable of leading those young enthusiasts.

Like Passy himself, most of his men were reservists, and as such, they knew very little about covert operations. Among those men, some are worth quoting: Sergeant Georges Lecot, who was known to have a difficult character, and Sergeant Jean Martin, for ever the discreet man; he became Passy's secretary. Also worthy of notes are Lieutenant Maurice Duclos, Russian-born Lieutenant Alexandre Beresnikoff who held a doctorate in law and could speak Russian, German, English and French or Raymond Lagier, who was born in a bourgeois family of Pontarlier and who had graduated in 1938 from the Ecole Supérieure de Commerce de Paris[2]. Among other valuable members of the team, one can also mention Captain André Manuel, who had been born in 1905. He linked-up with Passy in September

Bottom and following page, top.
Captain Pierre Billotte presenting General Ernest Petit the 185 men of the so-called "Russian" detachment on 9 September 1941. Many among those men volunteered for the SR but only 24 were eventually selected.
(ECPAD picture)

1. The FFI staff was formed from May 1944 with, among others, the Action and Operations sections of the BCRA. The operation suffered from strife between the French and the British secret services. Both organizations were also included in the command group of the FFI, which also fell under General Eisenhower's headquarters known as SHAEF (Supreme Headquarters Allied Expeditionary Forces), and under the special forces HQ known as the Special Forces Headquarters (SFHQ).

2. During the Norwegian campaign (from 9 April to 10 June 1940) the Allies attempted to seize the Norwegian ports that were under the control of German forces. The aim of this campaign was to prevent the delivery of the strategically important Swedish iron ore to the German armaments industry. The Allied commanders in Narvik, were General Mackesy, commander of British troops and General Béthouart, head of the French and Polish expeditionary force. The Allies had a total of 24,500 combatants reinforced by 5,000 Norwegians against about 5,200 German soldiers, 2,000 of them Alpine troops. In April, the battle for Narvik raged for four days leaving 343 dead within the Allied forces and nearly as many among the German troops. As for the Norwegian campaign, overall, it mobilized about 45,000 men on the Allied side and twice as much in the German side. The campaign resulted in the death of 2,400 men on the Allied side, (500 French) as well as 1,300 Norwegian, against nearly 5,300 Germans. If the battle of Narvik is sometimes considered, with the defence of the Alps against the Italian forces, as the only victory of the French army during the crucial years of 1939-1940 it did not prevent the Germans from occupying Norway.

1940 and he is considered as the co-founder of the BCRA. Another figurehead of the BCRA, was Captain Pierre Fourcaud from the Chasseurs Alpins (mountain rifles), a seasoned and motivated fighter, the only experienced intelligence operator who had developed his skills between the two world wars.

At this stage, the aim was to build a cohesive and reliable team. Charles de Gaulle did not want the Fighting French to be diluted within the British forces; he wanted them to fight alongsides their British comrades as representative of the new France for which he saw himself as the only guarantee. De Gaulle's determination on this matter was even stronger in 1943, against General Henri Giraud (1879-1949), who, in June 1943, co-chaired the French Committee of National Liberation (CFLN). It also showed the antagonism between de Gaulle and Giraud, the latter being preferred by the Americans and the British as he completely lacked any political sense.

In these early stages, the BCRA, has very little ressources.

However, following some successes and owing to the marked improvement in signal equipment, the British started to give more credit to the BCRA, which had been reorganized at end of 1941 and was steadily growing in strength. From October 1941, it was composed of four sections: intelligence gathering, direct action, evasions and general activities.

Recruitment continued to improve, the service attracting an increasing number of volunteers. From 23 members in November 1941, the BCRA went up to 77 members in July 1942, 119 in February

The trawler Jean-Charcot, one of the very first French ship to be used to ferry agents from the coast to British motorboats.
(Jean-Louis Le Bihon collection)

1943 and 350 (157 military and 193 civilians) in late 1943. During the same year, some new members like Stéphane Hessel, Jean Labaume, Bruno Larat, Tony Mella or Fred Scamaroni joined the BCRA. They were joined by other agents who had been compromised while in France and could no longer be deployed operationaly. Some examples of those compromised agents are known such as Edmond Pilat, a former member of the Musée de l'Homme network, who was posted to Section A, or Victor Attias and Paul Verdier, who arrived from North Africa as former members of an intelligence gathering network which was managed by the intelligence Service (IS). Verdier first went to R Section (intelligence) before being posted to CE Section (Counterintelligence).

Top.
General de Gaulle reviewing female Free French volunteers. A number of these women would eventually join the BCRA some as clerks, some as code specialists. Only a few would become agents or even saboteurs, such as Josiane and Marcelle Somers, Jeanne Bohec and Germaine Grüner.
(Fondation Charles de Gaulle picture)

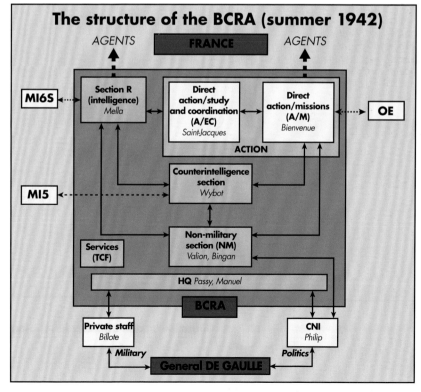

The structure of the BCRA (summer 1942)

AGENTS — FRANCE — AGENTS

MI6S ← → Section R (intelligence) *Mella* ← → Direct action/study and coordination (A/EC) *Saint-Jacques* ← → Direct action/missions (A/M) *Bienvenue* ← → OE

ACTION

Counterintelligence section *Wybot*

MI5 ← → Non-military section (NM) *Valion, Bingan*

Services (TCF)

HQ *Passy, Manuel*

BCRA

Private staff *Billote* — Military — General DE GAULLE — Politics — CNI *Philip*

Top.
During his May 1942 stay in London, Emmanuel d'Astier de la Vigerie had an argument with the BCRA leadership, which found its origin in his personal ambition. A year later, when in charge of the commissariat à l'Intérieur, he found Passy on his path when he tried to bring the Free French secret services under the authority of the Interior ministry.
(ECPAD picture)

Top.
Emmanuel d'Astier de la Vigerie a.k.a "Bernard". He belonged to the Libération-Sud network.
(François de Rochenoire collection picture)

BCRA's human potential continued to grow between 1943 and 1944; it is considered that Section R had some 200 agents deployed on various missions, the operational tempo picking up in the spring 1943. As for the Direct Action Service, it is estimated that between 200 and 250 missions were actually carried out [3].

As a first step, priority was given to intelligence gathering and the results obtained at the end of 1941 were quite satisfactory: nearly 910 pages divided into some 53 different packages had reached London, transiting through Spain thanks to covert networks established during the previous two years.

By the end of 1941, amateurism was a thing of the past in the BCRA... The system was now well established, even though danger remained.

The British had their own screening center located at the Royal Victorian Patriotic School (RVPS) also known as Patriotic School, on the outskirts of London. In order to detect possible German or Vichy agents, all the French escapees arriving in England had to transit there first to be questioned about their motivations and be given a clean bill of health by the counterintelligence specialists.

However, despite the selection at the Patriotic School carried out under the leadership of British military intelligence, MI5 (Military Intelligence, Section 5) followed by further screening at the Centre de Ralliement et d'Accueil (CRA, a temporary shelter for new french escapees), recruitment remained a weak point of the BCRA. At first, it did not meet up the expectations. It even contributed to the failure of some operations, because of unexperienced radio operators. When the BCRA tried to recruit radio operators from the Free French Naval Forces (FNFL), Vice Admiral Emile Muselier [4] (1882-1965), the head of the FNFL, quickly vetoed the proposition refusing to lose signal experts considered essential to the operational forces under his command.

By the end of 1942, the British had established and generalized a more stringent selection process for the agents. Additional tests were used; the services of a psychiatrist were introduced thus reducing the wastage rate from 10 to 1%. Simultaneously,

3. Sébastien Albertelli, *Les Services secrets du General de Gaulle. Le BCRA1940-1944*. Paris, éditions Perrin, 2010, page 146.
4. Emile Muselier is considered to have been the first general officer to have joined Charles de Gaulle in England at the end of June 1940. From the 1st of July 1940, he served as commander of the naval and air forces of Free France. But the disagreements between Giraudists and Gaullists put an end to the good relationship between General de Gaulle and Vice Admiral Muselier; from 1943, they went different ways.

the selection profile was modified in order to recruit stable men with a modest temperament, showing discipline and composure, quick-witted and skilled both in learning and restoring the newly taught techniques.

As already mentioned, the BCRA frequently changed name during the first months of its existence. Thus, it was called Service de Renseignements (Intelligence Service - SR) from 15 April 1941 [5]. The lack of resources limited its activity to the strict collection of data and intelligence and no operation was carried out.

In October 1941, four branches (called "sections") were created. These "sections" refer respectively to: General activities, under the command of Lieutenant de Boys, Intelligence, under the command of Captain Manuel André, Military Action, under the command of Captain Raymond Lagier (destruction of sensitive sites such as power stations, marshalling yards, railways and airports), and, Evasion (from France and North Africa in support of agents, individuals or even experts who absolutely had to reach London) - under the command of Captain Beresnikoff, and finally the coding section. Memo (2 464/SR) dated 16 December 1941, created a fifth section devoted to Counterintelligence (CI). Its mission was to screen the volunteers who wanted to join the Free French Forces. The CE section was under the command of Lieutenant Roger Warin, a.k.a "Wybot"; it worked closely with the "Special Branch" of Scotland Yard. Previous betrayals, such as the demise of Lieutenant de Vaisseau d'Estienne d'Orves who had been betrayed by his radio [6] had already proved that it was essential to protect the operational cells and networks deployed in France from enemy infiltration. Hence the efforts to detect enemy agents, traitors or "turned" French nationals. The British also had shown their ingenuity to find and discover German Abwehr agents infiltrated in England and their ability to "turn" them when possible using the double cross system [7].

In a few weeks, according to Passy, Wybot managed to create a file listing more than 100,000 persons in order to better manage and know the French nationals wishing to work in support of the Free

5. Note 1055-EMG signed on 12 april 1941 by General Petit, General de Gaulle's Chief-of-Staff, who was then in the Levant.
6. See page 42.
7. The management and handling of double agents working for the benefit of the British was the task of a specific service within MI5, called BIA.

Roger-Paul Warin *a.k.a "Wybot"*

In 1940, after the Fall of France, Warin, who then was a Lieutenant in the horse artillery, decided to remain in the Vichy armed forces after having been convinced by Colonel Groussard to work for the resistance. Warin then joined the Centre d'Informations et d'Etudes (Center for Information and Studies) which was eventually disbanded in late 1940.

Just like Warin, Groussard had decide to join the Gaullist in the United Kingdom. Warin was tasked with the penetration of the Marseille-based Bureau des menées anti-nationales (anti national activities bureau or BMA). He was specifically requested to provide intelligence on the anti-resistance activities of the BMA. From May 1941, he was in charge of BMA operations for the whole of the Marseille area. He had extensive contacts both with Allied and Gaullist agents. At the end of 1941 he reached the United Kingdom through Spain.

Taking advantage of his status as a BMA officer even though he was soon to be exposed, he decided to take leave from his employers in order to build another intelligence network before reaching London through Andorra, Spain and Portugal. Once in the UK, he joined the BCRA, heading the counterintelligence section where he established solid interrogation procedures and created a central intelligence registry.

Stanislas Mangin, son of General Mangin of World War one fame, then headed the network he had created in France.

After the liberation of France, Warin remained in the French intelligence community and co-participated in the creation of the Direction de la Surveillance du Territoire (Directorate for Territorial Surveillance or DST), which he directed from 1944 to 1959. Subsequently, he served as inspector general of the national security services and, from 1968, as the inspector general of the National Police services and schools. Finally, from 1969 to his retirement in 1973, he headed the general inspection and control services of the National Police.

During his career, Warin received the following decorations: *Commandeur de la Legion d'honneur,* Compagnon de la Libération (17 novembre 1945 decree), Croix de guerre 1939-1945 (with 4 citations), the King's Medal for Courage in the Cause of Freedom and he was made an Officer in the order of the Belgian crown.

(Archives Nationales picture)

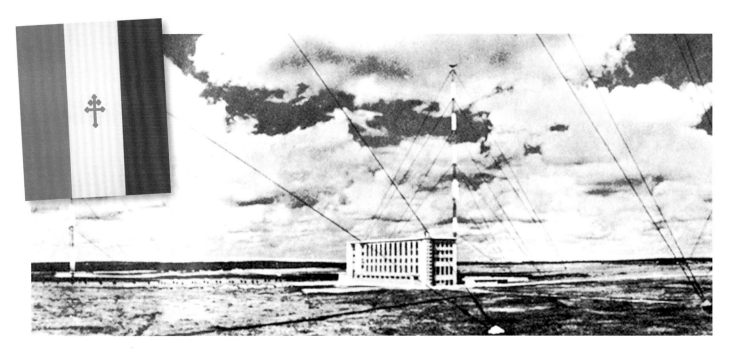

Top and Bottom.
During the night of 9 to 10 May 1942, after a parachute insertion from Great Britain, two French agents, Paul Bodhaine and Henri Clastère, blew up the aerial mast of Radio Paris in Allouis in the Cher département. They had previously been part of the "Russian" group which had joined Free France from the USSR under the command of Captain Pierre Billotte.
(Frédéric Vemon collection picture)

French Forces. Other sources refer to a list of about 60,000 people, which would have been used for counterintelligence[8] purposes.

SEVERAL OPERATIONAL CAPABILITIES

During this period, the British intelligence services showed remarkable operational capabilities. The Secret Intelligence Service (SIS), or MI6, established in 1909 focused on espionage, while the Special Operations Executive (SOE), founded in July 22, 1940 and disbanded in June 1946, carried out offensive and intelligence gathering missions and supported resistance networks in Europe[9]. To achieve these goals, the SOE relied on some French volunteers to carry out Direct Action missions. These volunteers were drawn from the 1st Compagnie de l'Air, a company-size Free French parachute unit which was located on the French training center at Exbury, in the New Forest (Hampshire County) on a land owned by the SOE and named Station 36 or Inchmery House. The center gradually became a selection, education, signal and sabotage training centre for the SOE.

Under General de Gaulle's guidance, Passy tried to counter the British recruitment drives among Free French volunteers. Even though they fought a

common enemy, there was a tense competition for talented Free French individuals between the SIS, the SOE and the "Deuxième Bureau" of the FFL.

Counterintelligence Section (CE) consists of nine members and was part of the Gaullists intelligence services. Warin established a central file designed to map out the French resistance. At the end of 1942, criticized for his authoritarianism and his questioning methods when screening French nationals who had escaped from occupied France, Roger Warin had to leave his position as head of the Counterintelligence Section (CE)[10]. Pierre Bloch who was later succeeded by François Thierry-Mieg replaced Warin[11].

Even before the Military action section of the SR had been created, Captain Raymond Lagier started recruiting volunteers among the officers and NCOs of the 1st Air infantry company which was then under the command of Captain Bergé, and from the young French FFL cadre from the Camberley training Center. Then, he divided the volunteers into three groups: organizers, saboteurs and radio operators. All had to follow the same training syllabus, based on the assimilation of commando techniques, demolition and weapons handling, as well as the hand-to-hand fighting, sabotage, the use of codes and the operation of signal equipment. Everyone received a code name. In total 11 missions were carried out by the SR in cooperation with SOE RF Section. At the end of 1941, 29 officers had been sent to France on behalf of the SR. Five of them were arrested or killed.

The SR was organized in two branches. The first was dedicated to intelligence gathering and

8. Robert Belot, Gilbert Karpman, "La circulation du renseignement clandestin dans la résistance: enjeux politiques et techniques de la cryptographie", in Fabienne Mercier-Bernadet (dir.), *1939-1945; La guerre des intelligences.* Paris, éditions Lavauzelle, Collection "Renseignements et guerre secrète", 2002, page 394.
9. The SOE, rival of MI6 (*Military Intelligence*, Section 6–MI6), was directly under the British Minister of Economic Warfare, Hugh Dalton. SOE is finally absorbed by MI6 in 1946.
10. The creation of a CE section was made necessary to stop the tide of arrests which seriously disrupted the activities of the covert networks in France.
11. The name of BCRA was proposed by Warin. At the end of the war, he also proposed the creation of the Directorate of Territorial Surveillance (DST - *Direction de la Surveillance du Territoire*) - created by the Order of 16 November, 1944 - and he run it until 1959. According to the Article 1 of the Decree of 22 November 1944 D.8017/SN/ST, the main functions of the DST then were to carry on research and centralization of the Counterintelligence intelligence, for future analysis by the Ministry of Interior; air and radio communications security, including the identification and suppression of covert actvities, the fight against covert air transport, and finally the punishment of offenses subject to the decree of 29 July, 1939.

Jacques Bingen

Jacques Bingen, who was André Citroën's brother-in-law, stemmed from a Jewish family of Italian origin. He graduated in political sciences, in addition to being a former pupil of the prestigious Ecole des Mines.

He fulfilled his military obligations in 1930-1931 as an artillery officer. He was then mobilized in 1939 as a reserve Lieutenant and became a liaison officer with the British 51st (Highland) Infantry Division. Wounded in June 1940 in the Haute-Normandie region, he was finally evacuated by train to La Rochelle, where he learnt about the armistice. Refusing to admit defeat, he decided to reach England (through Casablanca and Gibraltar), where he arrived in early July 1940, posing as a Polish officer. He arrived in Liverpool 18 July 1940. A few days later, he joined the entourage of Charles de Gaulle, who, in August, appointed him as Head of the Free French merchant navy. He remained in this position until October 1941, when he resigned, as a result of strong disagreement with Vice Admiral Muselier. He then became National Commissioner for the navy and the merchant navy in the French National Committee.

In November 1941, he was appointed as Deputy Manager of the North Africa Service within the National Commissioner of the Interior office before finally joining the BCRA in 1942. He was put in charge of the civilian aspects of the links with the resistance within occupied France.

Following the arrest of Jean Moulin, in June 1943, he, from mid-August 1943, became the delegate representing the French Committee of National Liberation to the internal resistance of the French South Zone. Facing the potential fraction of the Résistance into various sub groups, Jacques Bingen is among those who worked to preserve a certain unity, in line with what Jean Moulin had done. He worked to unify the military and paramilitary resistance movements and established the Finance Committee. He also took an important part in the structuring of the National Council of Resistance.

After returning to London, he returned to the South of France, but was arrested by the Gestapo on 12 May 1944, in Clermont-Ferrand. He had been betrayed by a double agent, Alfred Dormal, who operated for the German intelligence (Abwehr). At the age of 36, he chose to swallow his cyanide capsule rather than to take the risk of giving away vital information under torture.

He was made a Companion of the Liberation and was awarded the Legion d'honneur. His body has never been found.

Left.
Jacques Bingen (pictured here as a First Lieutenant in 1939) headed the delegation which represented General de Gaulle to the Résistance within occupied France from September 1943 to April 1944.
(Musée de l'Ordre de la Libération picture)

targeting in support of air raids: airfields, ports, oil refineries, etc. When considered urgent, the intelligence reports were generally transmitted by radio. If not, they were sent by mail, transiting through Spain and Switzerland. The other branch of the SR was focused on operations with delayed results such as the preparation of sabotage operations. The idea was to create a network of supporters who would, when ordered, be prepared to support allied operations.

Repeatedly, General de Gaulle expressed his strong desire to dissociate intelligence gathering and direct action missions. Such an order was often difficult to obey in the field, far away from the general staff. After the war, many members of the resistance complained of having received inappropriate orders and instructions from London that did not fit at all with the dangerous reality they were then facing.

While the FFL's networking operations got organized in Africa, Passy named André Manuel as Deputy of the "Deuxième Bureau". He was a balloonist reserve officer, then 35 years old. He held this position for four years. A stickler for regulations, Admiral Muselier who was then senior commander of Free French forces in Britain, did not care much for the "Deuxième Bureau" unorthodox ways. He thus did everything he could to complicate the existence of this service. In order to calm things down and because of the urgent nature of Admiral Muselier's demands, Passy accepted that the Deuxième Bureau was to be placed under the command of a naval officer. Lieutenant Commander d'Estienne d'Orves, a graduate from the prestigious Polytechnique School thus became the commander of the Deuxième Bureau and, at the same time, a secret agent code-named "Chateauvieux". In due time, Muselier's obstrusive behaviour and his attempt

at controlling services that did not fall under his command owed him a severe rebuke from General de Gaulle.

The new service that Passy tried to build in full compliance to de Gaulle's [12] orders nevertheless had to face rumors that tarnished the image and credibility of what was to become the BCRA. It was then rumoured that the Deuxième Bureau was full of fascists attached to the Secret Organization of Revolutionary Action (SRC), also known as "La Cagoule" (The Hood) [13].

Despite Passy's efforts, the rumour persisted until after the war. In fact, the BCRA was mostly

Top.
Jedburgh drawing their kit before an operational mission.
(US National Archives picture)

UN SEUL COMBAT
POUR UNE SEULE PATRIE

12. This right-wing movement emerged in 1935 from a rupture between the National Revolutionary Party (PNR) and the Action Française.
13. La Cagoule was headed by Eugene Deloncle. It was fundamentally anti-semitic, anti-communist and supporter of subversive actions. The movement was disbanded by the Ministry of the Interior at the end of 1937. Most of its former members joined in time the Vichy regime but some refused collaboration and joined resistance movements

a conglomerate of people driven by ideals similar to socialism. The BCRA even managed, during a pick-up operation, to bring back to London Charles Vallin, President of the French Socialist Party (Parti Socialiste Français - PSF), and a Major collaborator of Colonel François de La Rocque, at the request of General de Gaulle who wanted to demonstrate the FFL ability to recruit on all sides of the political spectrum. For the anti-Gaullists, it was interpreted as hard evidence of his favorable attention towards the fascists. The BCRA also recruited men like Jean Pierre-Bloch, who was, at that time, a Socialist member of the parliament in the Aisne department, who had left the SOE to join the BCRA, or men like Pierre Brossolette or Louis Vallon. This is a far cry from the persistent post-war image of a fascist group, although some of its members were more or less close to "La Cagoule [14]." André Labarthe, an anti-Gaullist to the core and the editor of the La France Libre magazine, launched this allegation.

From 17 January 1942, the service changed its name and became the Central Bureau of Intelligence and Military Operations (Bureau central de renseignements et d'action militaire - BCRAM), while being at the same time integrated into the personal staff of General de Gaulle [15]. From then on, it consisted of five sections including the Command group headed by Passy, and it had 53 members on strength. The other sections were respectively in charge of intelligence (Section R), under the command of Captain André Manuel also known as "Pallas". Its mission was to control the preparation of missions, to recruit agents and to liaise with the IS. The military action (Section AM) was placed under the command of Captain Lagier. In connection with the operations' desk, its mission was to select and train the agents tasked with the destruction of military targets. It was

in contact with the SOE. The counterintelligence (Section EC) was under the command of Lieutenant Warin, a.k.a "Wybot". A section devoted to Technology, Encryption and Finance (Section TCF) under the command of Lieutenant Drouot was in charge of the financial and technical issues, as well as of training in the use of codes, encryption and decryption of letters and other messages for the benefit of the staff.

In 1942, the BCRA, all sections included, numbered 53 people, including 17 officers.

The creation of the Research and Coordination Section (Section A / EC) from 23 March 1942 (memo 307/BCRAM), answered a typically French logic, which aims at permanently expanding any administrative structure. This Section worked in close connection with the AM Section (Military Action) for the development of global action plans and the compartmentalization of France in the operating field. Section A / EC was entrusted to "Saint-Jacques." In February 1942 [16], the Evasion Section (Section E) was under the command of Lieutenant Mitchell and it was restructured in order to operate more closely with MI9 [17].

In addition to this internal architecture, the Documentation and Dissemination section (Section DD), was established in July 1942 [18] and, finally, the nonmilitary Section (Section N / M) which focused on political actions inside France in connection with the French resistance. Practically, this meant sending mails, propaganda leaflets or guidelines for political mission [19].

The designation of BCRA was adopted on 1 September 1942; it stuck and pushed all the others into oblivion.

The Service Afrique du Nord (North Africa Service) which had previously been part of the Commissioner of the Interior, was then incorporated into the BCRA.

---

14. Major Duclos, a.k.a "Saint-Jacques" was one proven member of La Cagoule; Lieutenant Colonel Fourcaud was known to be a sympathizer.
15. The private staff of Charles de Gaulle was activated on September 1941.
16. The Evasion Section was set up in October 1941 but it was temporarily managed by the Commissioner of the Interior. From 27 June 1942, it belonged entirely to the BCRA.
17. Established at the end of 1940, Military Intelligence (Department 9) was part of the War Office; it was integrated to the Directorate of Military Intelligence. The task of MI9 was to support the exfiltration towards the UK of pilots who had been downed in hostile areas but also of resistants and escaped POWs.
18. The DD Section was reorganized in 1943 into two sub-sections created respectively in the NEC and N / M Sections.
19. Result of yet another administrative reorganization, Section N / M is eventually absorbed on 10 January, 1944, by the mail, documentation and broadcasting service (SCDD) of the Commissioner of the Interior, itself created on 10 January 1944.

Top left.
Raymond Lagier was recruited by Passy in London. They had fought in Norway together in 1940. Under the alias of "Bienvenüe", he set up the Action section in June 1941; he remained in command of it until the Spring of 1943.
(Archives Nationales picture)

Top right.
General Cochet, who had been one of the first to join the Résistance and to reach London soon clashed with Passy. Even though he was appointed head of the Free French intelligence and action services in October 1943, he never managed to take control of the BCRA.
(ECPAD picture)

THE BCRA THROUGH ITS VARIOUS SECTIONS

INTELLIGENCE SECTION (R–Renseignement): This section was intended to prepare the intelligence-gathering mission, as well as to establish recruitment programs and the preparation and execution of missions. Finally, it was to liaise with the British Intelligence Agency (MI6). Captain André Manuel, Tony Mella and Jean Fleury commanded it.

Military Action Section (A/M): established on 10 October 1941, it was under the command of Captain Raymond Lagier, a.k.a "Bienvenüe", Fred Scamaroni, Jacques Robert a.k.a "Rewez" and Pierre Lejeune. Its task was to train the agents in charge of the destruction of military targets it had itself selected in partnership with the SOE (RF Section). Those targets were synchronized with the courses of action developed in conjunction with General de Gaulle's staff.

Escape Section (E): established on 10 October 1941 as well, this section was under the command of Lieutenant Roger Mitchell, a.k.a "Brick". Its mission was to organize and ensure the escape and evasion out of the French territory of POWs on the run or compromised agents. The section worked in partnership with the British MI9. Mitchell made many trips between England, Spain and Portugal to ensure the return of compromised agents, POWs on the run or downed Allied pilots.

Encryption and then Technical, Encryption and Finance Section (TCF) initially established on 10 October 1941, according to a first draft, it evolved into a section of financial and technical management of the BCRA on the one hand, and, on the other into a training element dedicated to the task of teaching codes and cyphers. The Section TCF was under the command of Georges Lecot a.k.a "Drouot".

Counterintelligence Section (EC): It was added to the previous sections, a few months later on

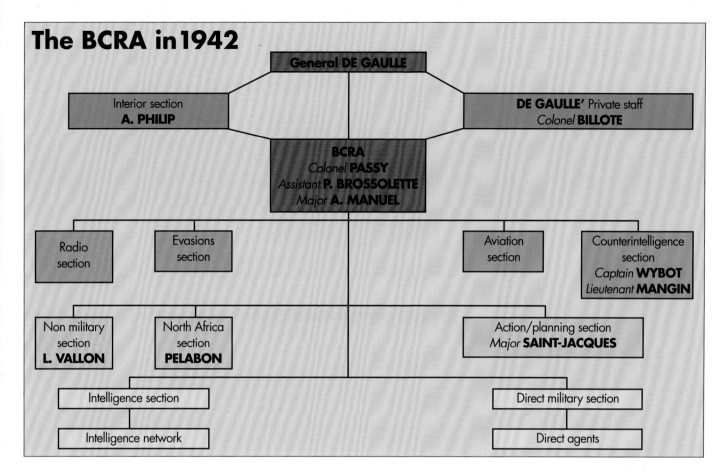

The BCRA in 1942

General DE GAULLE

| Interior section **A. PHILIP** | | **DE GAULLE'** Private staff *Colonel* **BILLOTE** |

BCRA
Colonel **PASSY**
Assistant **P. BROSSOLETTE**
Major **A. MANUEL**

- Radio section
- Evasions section
- Aviation section
- Counterintelligence section *Captain* **WYBOT** *Lieutenant* **MANGIN**

- Non military section **L. VALLON**
- North Africa section **PELABON**
- Action/planning section *Major* **SAINT-JACQUES**

- Intelligence section
  - Intelligence network
- Direct military section
  - Direct agents

---

16 December 1941. It was initially under the command of Roger Warin (code name "Wybot") and Stanislas Mangin, then of Major Bonnefous from 1943 on. This Section had to ensure that the BCRA was not being infiltrated. It also struggled against the infiltration of resistance networks located in France. To this purpose after having carefully interviewed and grilled them, it kept a central file of all the French nationals who had landed in the United Kingdom, in conjunction with the Security Service. At the very end of the conflict, it became urgent to recruit extra agents to grow the numbers of the DGSS (General Directorate for Special Services), which became the SDECE in 1946. The rigor of the screening was then found to be lacking by some French nationals seeking professional opportunities and who did not hesitate to pose as resistance fighters.

Studies and Coordination Section (A / EC): It was responsible for the preparation of raids and sabotage against strategic German installations. Established on 28 March 1942, this Section experienced various changes in the following years, as it was first integrated to the Military Action Section (A / M), before becoming a separate entity of the BCRA. It was placed under the command of Maurice Duclos a.k.a "Saint-Jacques".

Documentation and Dissemination Section (DD): In view of the increasing administrative needs of the BCRA, this section was established on July 3 1942, as a special section for intelligence and information management (sorting and selection of intelligence reports, distribution and dissemination according to importance, urgency, etc.)…

Political Section (this section was called the "Section Non Militaire" or N / M): Section N / M was akin to Section DD for the gathering of political intelligence. It worked in close collaboration with the Section Renseignement, the Commissariat à l'intérieur (Office of the Interior) and the agents of Section A / M, who, when they returned from their missions, provided regular non-military intelligence updates. The political choices and procedures decided in London by the various Free French authorities (in particular by the Commissariat à l'intérieur) were then transmitted in an encrypted form to the resistance networks in France through Section A / M agents. Given its close relationship with the Commissariat à l'intérieur, Section N / M was eventually integrated into the BCRA as the mail-documentation-diffusion service (SCDD) as of January 1944.

Top.
Jack Mansion OBE was the first Free French agent to have landed in France, in the Finistère département, in July 1940. Within two months and with the help of fishermen from the village of Bénodet, he managed to bring back to the United Kingdom a number of maps depicting the German order of Battle in Brittany.
(Musée de l'ordre de la Libération picture)

André Manuel a.k.a "Pallas"

Manuel, whose family was linked to the textile industry in the area of Epinal, was a textile engineer by training. In 1940, he was a Lieutenant qualified as a balloonist. He reached Liverpool in July 1940 and joined the *Forces Francaises Libres* two days after his arrival, on July 15, 1940. After a stint as a logistics officer, he was posted to the intelligence branch of the Free French staff. Subsequently, he became the head of the intelligence cell of the secret services and became a close aide to Passy until the end of the conflict.

At the end of 1942, he led an important mission (Mission Pallas) which aimed at improving the organization - and the Free French control over them – of the intelligence networks located in France. André Manuel remained on French soil from the night of 22 to 23 November 1942 to the night of January 26 to 27, 1943.

He remained involved with secret services after the war, serving both with the Direction Generale des Services Spéciaux (DGSS) and the Service de Documentation Extérieure et de Contre Espionnage (SDECE)

Top.
One of the very few pictures depicting André Manuel. He is seen here on a British ship returning to France in August 1944. He is surrounded by British officers and by Captain Landrieux.
(Musée du Plan Sussex collection)

In order to facilitate the relations between the different French structures that revolved around General de Gaulle, the COLI was established on 10 February 1943, with the task of ensuring a permanent connection between the BCRA and Colonel Pierre Billotte (1906 - 1992)[1], Air Marshal François d'Astier de La Vigerie (1888-1956), a fighter pilot who joined the resistance in 1940[2] and André Philip (1902-1970), then Commissioner of the Interior. All joined de Gaulle in London in 1942. According to Jean-Louis Cremieux-Brilhac, Billotte was considered the administrative and military controller of the BCRA and he was the liaison officer between the service and Charles de Gaulle[3].

At the end of September 1943, the BCRA created a "Staff and Services" Section (Section EM / S), placed under the command of Captain Landrieux, whose task was to manage the staff, infrastructure and logistics of the Service.

Then, on 6 October 1943, a Code Section was created, under the command of Lieutenant Stephenson. This section was in charge of encryption (encoding and decoding letters, telegrams, etc.).

Daily, at 6pm, the officers in command of the different sections gathered around Passy and updated him on the messages they had received during the day while he briefed them on his directions and guidances. Through the BCRA, Pierre Billotte played an important role in directing the operations led by the FFL (Forces Françaises Libres – Free French Forces) in direct liaison with the resistance within occupied France. From December 1942 on, he also was the secretary of the Comité Militaire Permanent (Permanent Military Committee) and in May 1943, of the Comité de Défense Nationale (Committee on National Defence) based in Algiers

In early 1943, the BCRA has reached its cruising speed and its organization was well established. In early 1942, the new service had a strength of 53; in the first months of 1943 it had grown to 151 to reach 350 by the end of 1943 (157 military, 193 civilians) all based in London [4]. However, the anti-gaullists were still trying to tarnish the image of the BCRA, presenting it as a Gestapo-like organization. The suicide of a compromised German infiltrated agent in the premises of the BCRA, in Duke Street, in February 1943, helped to spread the rumor that the BCRA agents employed brutal interrogation methods comparable to those used by the enemy. The case was known and leaked to Washington, especially by known anti-Gaullists U.S. officials. In August 1943, the testimony of Maurice Dufour accentuated the rumour. The latter alleged that, in 1942, members of the BCRA counterintelligence section had tortured him. He even lodged a complaint against de Gaulle and Passy, requesting the British judicial system to intervene. In fact, Dufour had pretended to be an officer in the Engineer Corps and to have been decorated with the prestigious cross of chevalier de la Légion d'Honneur; he also had accepted to work for the British and American services in order to escape a conviction in absentia for 10 years in prison for the illegal wearing of a decoration and military rank he did not hold. Finally, while the case against de Gaulle and the BCRA officers was supposed to begin in June 1944, the British Prime Minister stopped the legal proceedings.

Since the BCRA sent more and more agents on operational missions, each had to be given a "nom-de-guerre" in order to hide their true identities while at the same time protecting their families that for the Majority remained in occupied France. The "nom-de-guerre" were names of metro stations in Paris, more specifically of line 6. As already mentionned, Dewavrin became "Passy" Fourcaud went for "Barbes", "Lucas" Beresnikoff selected "Corvisart" and Duclos "Saint-Jacques." Lagier became "Bienvenue".

Top.
On the right, French Air Force General François d'Astier de la Vigerie DFC, compagnon de la Libération. Called to London by de Gaulle, he managed, after a number of attempts, to reach England by Lysander on 18 November 1942.
(ECPAD picture)

1. Captured in June 1940 in the area of Mourmelon during the Battle of France, Pierre Billotte was first kept as a POW in Pomerania. He escaped and made his way to the USSR in February 1941. After a few months of internment, the Soviets wrongly suspecting him of being a spy, he managed to convince them to allow him to return to the UK. He reached Great-Britain on 9 September 1941 with approximately 185 other Free French volunteers. Billotte first served in the personal staff of General de Gaulle, then in May 1942, as he had been promoted to the rank of Lieutenant-Colonel in December 1941, he was appointed head of the personal staff of General de Gaulle.
2. Under a decree of the Free France dated 1 December 1942, General d'Astier was appointed Deputy to General de Gaulle, commander of the Free French Forces and member of the High Military Committee. His brother Henri d'Astier (1897-1952), a royalist and a patriot, he provided valuable intelligence on Luftwaffe units located in Normandy. He established the Orion network. Emmanuel d'Astier (1900-1969), who just like his two older brothers also became a Compagnion de la Libération, was, in January 1942, at the origin of the "Libération" group and newspaper that operated in the South Zone. He created "Libération" a few months after another group he had created in Cannes called "*La Dernière Colonne*" had been decimated.
3. Jean-Louis Crémieux-Brilhac, *La France libre. De l'appel du 18 juin à la Libération*. Paris, éditions Gallimard, 1996, page 387.
4. Guy Perrier, *Le colonel Passy et les services secrets de la France libre*. Paris, éditions Hachette Littératures, 1999, page 178.

The secret services of General de Gaulle: a constant change of name

1 July 1940-14 April 1941: *Deuxième Bureau*
15 April 1941-16 January 1942: *Service de Renseignement* (SR)
17 January 1942-31 August 1942: *Bureau Central de Renseignements et d'Action Militaire* (BCRAM)
1 September 1942: *Bureau Central de Renseignements et d'Action* (BCRA)
4 October 1943: Strengthening of the ties between the BCRA and *Service de Renseignement et d'Action* (SRA) located in Algiers
19 November 1943: Creation of the *Direction Générale des Services Spéciaux* (DGSS) which integrated the London – based *Bureau du Renseignement et d'Action de Londres* (BRAL) – the BCRA remaining independent of this structure and the Algiers – based *Bureau du Renseignement et d'Action d'Alger* (BRAA)

Top.
The RAF jump school in Ringway. The training apparatus were designed by RAF Flight Lieutenant John C. Kilkenny. All Free French agents had to go through this school in order to get their parachute wings.
(Public Archives of Canada picture)

Right.
Escape and Evasion silk map. They were issued to allied aircrews.
(François de Rochenoire collection picture)

Most French escapees from the continent or even from North Africa preferred to fight in more conventional structures. Therefore, it was difficult for Passy to find volunteers for covert action. He made sure that every single new escapee went through the Deuxième Bureau offices in order to get from them an updated intelligence picture of the situation in France. This method allowed him to recruit some new elements, including Gilbert Renault, who became "Roulier" or "Rémy". Originally a film producer by trade, he opened up a host of new opportunities to Passy thanks to all his professional connections that were still active in occupied France.

The BCRA Operations desk mostly relied on the Renseignement (intelligence, known as Section R) and Action Militaire (military action, known as Section AM) sections. Section R worked closely with the Secret Intelligence Service (SIS) as well as the SOE. The British mastery of covert operations was undeniable. Sections N / M & A also worked with the SOE, which supplied weapons and the logistics in support of guerrilla operations[6]. The contact between Section A and SOE were established through RF Section, which was under the command of Lieutenant Colonel Hutchinson. Since the French depended on the British for their logistic and financial support, the RF section focused on training, equipment

Top.
Agent training included
fieldcraft and land
navigation exercises. Still
from a documentary on SOE
agents training.
(François de Rochenoire
collection picture)

and transportation of French Intelligence Service agents. In addition to RF Section, SOE also had, in France, Section F, which, unlike the RF, operated autonomously and without any connection with Free France agents. Passy and the rest of the BCRA only learnt of the existence of Section F much later in the war. Section F only openly worked with the French from May 1944 on.

The Direct Action Section of the BCRA, just like the French Section of SOE operated according to the same logic: to support resistance movements in occupied areas and provide them with operational support. The French Section of the SOE was organized in two branches: the first, known as Section F was placed under the command of Colonel Maurice Buckmaster (1902-1992). Operating totally independently from the French, something which was strongly resented by de Gaulle and Passy[7]. The other branch, called RF Section, was composed of some of the best known shadow warriors of those dark times such as Colonel Hutchinson DSO, Forest Frederick Edward Yeo-Thomas GC, MC & Bar (1902-1964) a.k.a "White Rabbit" or Captain Eric Wicks-Picquet. It liaised between the BCRA and the SOE.

The Counterintelligence Section had a link to MI5 (Military Intelligence, Section 5) which focused on Counterintelligence and the protection of the British territory, while Section E was connected to MI9 which had been established in December 1940 and was placed under the command of Colonel Norman Crockatt. MI9's mission was the recovery and the support of Résistance fighters, war prisoners or downed pilots in order to help them escape from the occupied territories to the United Kingdom.

CNI AND BCRA:
OVERLAP AND TEMPORARY CONFUSION

When the Commissariat National à l'Intérieur (National Commissioner of the Interior or CNI) decided it wanted to give a go at covert actions, it created tensions with the BCRA as the CNI's aim was to centralize all the agents in charge of gathering political or economic intelligence.

General de Gaulle's order to separate intelligence and direct action contributed to mission overlapp between the BCRA and the CNI even though they all tended to aim for the same effects, in the military or in the political fields. Because of a lack of coordination, this caused some confusion, which was of course not helped by the complete misun-

6. At the end of 1942, the SOE had two squadrons based in Tempsford: N°138 Squadron (Halifax) and N°161 Squadron (Halifax, Lysander and Hudson).
7. The action of Buckmaster was nevertheless recognized has having been of invaluable military value. De Gaulle's criticism were that he had sometimes acted in opposition to French interests, that he had recruited both anti-Gaullist and Gaullist without any distinction and, especially, that he had favoured the Communists by providing weapons to the *Francs-tireurs et partisans français* (FTPF).

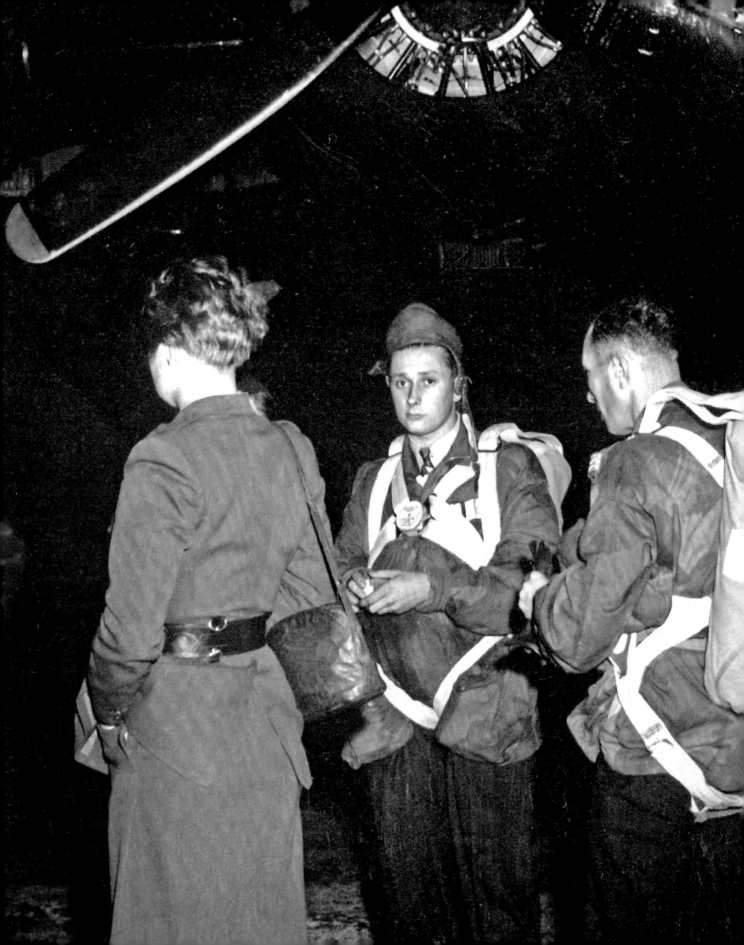

derstanding, which bordered on hostility displayed by the CNI against the BCRA.

Finally, after several months and under the leadership of Passy who demanded a solution, General de Gaulle decided that the BCRA was no longer confined to military missions and he authorized the service to establish its own political action service. On 4 August 1942, a non-military section (N / M) was created and placed under the command of Louis Vallon (1901-1981), a Polytechnique school graduate and former member of the Section Française de l'Internationale Ouvrière (French Section of the Workers' International or SFIO), and of his Deputy Jacques Bingen (1908-1944), whose crucial role is, even today, often downplayed in the collective memory.

Following Passy's request, all BCRA members had to be parachute trained. Thus, they had to perform the seven mandatory jumps of the Parachute Landing School in Ringway, Scotland.

Each member also had to carry out a mission in France, both for the sake of credibility and for each agent to be fully aware of the risks taken by the agents deployed on operations. To be sent on a mission, the officers had to volunteer; among the sixty London-based officers with command responsibilities within the BCRA, fourteen were actually sent out on a mission; six of them died. The Majority of these missions were conducted between October 1942 and May 1943[8].

Initially located on St. James's Square, the BCRA moved to 10, Duke Street in 1942 in order to face an increase in its strength.

The years 1940-1942 were crucial in establishing links between the London-based BCRA and the freshly established but growing covert networks in occupied France. From 1942 on, the reports sent to the Free French structures in London help map out the importance of the underground networks. With the help of this intimate knowledge of the French underground networks, the secret services of General de Gaulle could organize and synchronize the operations assigned to the different resistance groups. The idea was to achieve the unification of the Résistance elements that were not placed under a single command at the time. The creation of the Conseil National de la Résistance (National Council of Resistance, CNR), which held its first meeting on 27 May 1943, was meant to answer that need.

Left.
The "Aubrey" Jedburgh team in front of B 24 D-42-40506-R Fightin'Sam (piloted by an American officier named Moser). This team was to be parachuted during operation "Spiritualist 6" on 12 August over le Plessis- Belleville. Left to right: a WAAF with her back to the camera, Ivor Alfred Hooker "Thaler" a British radio operator, and Free French Lieutenant Adrien Chaigneau "Koldare" a.k.a J. Telmon who was killed on 27 August 1944 near Oissery.
(US National Archives picture)

---

8. Sébastien Albertelli, *Les Services secrets du General de Gaulle. Le BCRA 1940-1944.* Paris, éditions Perrin, 2010, 617 pages.

1943
TOWARDS THE UNIFICATION OF THE FRENCH SECRET SERVICE

THE END OF 1942 and the beginning of 1943 coincided with the real rise of the Free French secret services. From then on, the BCRA demonstrated its capacity to recruit and train its own agents without having to totally depend on the British as it was previously.

THE TENSIONS BETWEEN DE GAULLE AND GIRAUD

After the Allied landings in North Africa (8 November 1942, Operation Torch), the question of the real weight of the Free French influence over the Allies particularly in the Maghreb area, became a very important issue. For de Gaulle, the situation was difficult. He had to make his presence felt decisively if he did not want to die politically, particularly when dealing with the Americans.

Another issue was the reliability of the Vichy senior civil servants who had only fled to North Africa after Operation Torch or after the occupation of the free zone by the Germans in November 1942. Several senior officials of the Vichy armed forces *Service de Renseignement* (Intelligence Service, SR) had gone to Algiers. Among them were Colonel Rivet, Captain Paul Paillole, Lieutenant Commander Trautmann from the SR Marine (Navy Intelligence) and Colonel Ronin. Until then, all had been working for the Vichy authorities of Philippe Pétain but

they had cooperated with the Intelligence Service in 1939-1940. Not being Gaullists, they placed themselves under the commandment of General Giraud and contributed to the creation of the *Direction des Services de Renseignement et de la Sécurité Militaire* (Directorate of Intelligence and Military Security or DSR-SM) placed under the command of Colonel Rivet[1]. Then, from April 1943, a *Direction des Services Spéciaux* (Directorate of Special Services or DSM) was set up. It incorporated the DSR-SM as well as a direct action service and it was placed under the command of Ronin, who had been promoted to the rank of general in the meantime.

Charles de Gaulle clashed with Giraud who, initially, abided by the Vichy laws and did not hesitate to arrest Gaullist sympathizer in southern Algeria. Then, under the influence of Jean Monnet, Giraud adopted the republican principles and broke away from Vichy.

Everything set apart the two men: two strong and quite conceited characters, and the memories of past tensions[2]. Nothing could bring the two men together. De Gaulle positioned himself as a providential figurehead for the new France to come; Giraud did not share his view and he gathered around him some of the French intelligence specialists who had broken away from the Vichy regime and who had chosen not to support the rise of the gaullist Intelligence Service. De Gaulle's cold character, his quest for supremacy, his controlling and dominating demeanor and what is sometimes perceived as a lack of humility certainly played a role on the way he was perceived by some. This in no way detracts from his exceptional skills and his ability to analyze a situation and identify problems.

The circumstances of the war dictated a political rapprochement even though the secret services of Charles de Gaulle and Henri Giraud were still in competition. The French secret services had to show a unified face to the Allies. An end had to be put to the strife between Giraudists and Gaullists.

From Algiers, General Giraud managed his special services that were mainly composed of former members of the Vichy military intelligence services placed under the command of General Ronin. These services were made up of a *Service de Renseignement* (intelligence service or SR), which was placed under the command of Colonel Rivet, and of a *Service de Contre-Espionnage et de Sécurité Militaire* (counterintelligence and military security service or CESM), placed under the command of Major Paul Paillole. They had points of contact in London: Lieutenant-Colonel Berroeta for the SR, Lieutenant Commander Bonnefous for the CE and Major Lejeune, who managed the agents earmarked for operational missions.

Operational areas within France were divided between the different services. London-based service were in charge of operations in the North, Northeast, East and Southwest of France, while Algiers focused on operations carried out in the South and Southeast of the country.

It is not difficult to imagine the in fighting that resulted from the synchronisation and unification of the various French services disseminated between the United Kingdom and French North Africa. Despite his misgivings, on 19 May 1943, Giraud gave his agreement to the establishment of an Executive Committee he co-chaired with de

(continued on page 40)

1. From 4 January 1943, Major military security of the DSR-SM was entrusted to the commander Paillole.
2. In 1936, General Giraud was at the head of the 7th Army and member of the Supreme Council of War, when Colonel Charles de Gaulle advocated the development of the armoured corps within the French army. However, Giraud refuted the thesis of de Gaulle.

The N 51 (Le Dinan), which was Captained by Peter Fryer. This ship did several return trips between France and the United Kingdom during the war.
(Jean-Louis Le Bihon collection)

Gilbert Renault

a.k.a "Rémy"

Gilbert Renault was born in Vannes in Brittany, where he completed his secondary studies at the Collège Saint-François-Xavier before reading Law in the city of Rennes.

During the second half of the 1930s, he tried his hand at banking and at film production without meeting with much success. Nevertheless, he drew a vast network of contacts from that period that would prove very useful during the Second World War.

In August 1940, he set up, in collaboration with Louis de La Bardonnie, a Résistance network called the Confrérie Notre Dame (the Brotherhood of Our Lady), which, three years later would become the Confrérie Notre Dame-Castille (Brotherhood of Our Lady- Castille). This network remained one of the largest resistance networks ever to have operated in France. It was virtually destroyed on several occasions and it fielded over 1,500 agents.

Considered as one of the most faithful secret agents of General de Gaulle - he was made a Companion of the Liberation by a decree of March 13, 1942,

"Rémy" had several other noms-de-guerre, including, "Raymond", "Morin", "Watteau", "Ro" and "Beauce". In 1950, his position in favor of the rehabilitation of Marshal Philippe Pétain led to his sidelining by General de Gaulle.

He left an impressive bibliography (nearly thirty books), including his Mémoires d'un agent secret de la France libre (Memoirs of a Secret Agent of Free France) as well as many articles.

His decorations included the Cross of Commander of the Legion honor, the Croix de guerre 1939-1945, the Medaille de la Résistance with Rosette, the Distinguished Service Order, the cross of Officer of the Order of the British Empire, the belgian Croix de guerre, the title of officer of the Belgian Crown, the Cross of Commandeur du Mérite from Luxembourg and the cross of Officer of the Legion of Merit from the United States.

Top.
Gilbert Renault, a.k.a Colonel Rémy parading in the streets of Vannes with General de Gaulle in July 1946.
(Louis Royère collection picture)

Previous page Top.
A series of pictures of Rémy, his spouse and children as well as Daniel Lomenech on board the N 51 heading towards the United Kingdom in June 1942 after the Marie-Louise mission.
(Renault family picture)

Previous page bottom right.
Forged identity documents belonging to Rémy.
(Renault family picture)

Top.
Gilbert Renault a.k.a "Rémy" who had become Colonel Rémy by the end of the War.
(Musée de l'ordre de la Libération picture)

Rémy returning to France onboard a trawler in September 1942. On this particular trip, the link up with the reception committee failed. A second attempt was done three weeks later, ending up on a success.
(Renault family picture)

Top.
Having distinguished himself during the Battle of France in May-June 1940, Jean Assemat joined the Free French Forces in London. After completing parachute training in Ringway in February 1944, he was posted to the BCRA. Within the frame of Plan Proust, he was seconded, under the alias of Jacques Bauer, to the Office of Strategic Services. On 12 July 1944, he was parachuted over Douadic, South of Blanc in the Indre département. Jean Assemat remained with the airborne forces for the rest of his military career, later seeing action in Indochina and Algeria.
(Musée des troupes aéroportées de Pau picture)

Top.
Jean Assemat a.k.a Jacques Bauer FFI stamp.
(Archives Nationales document)

Bottom.
Cyanide pill and parachute riser of Jean Assemat a.k.a "Jacques Bauer", a.k.a "Ulm".
(Musée de la Poche de Royan collection)

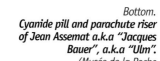

Gaulle. Then, in June 1943[3], under Giraud, the Comité Français de Libération Nationale (French Committee of National Liberation or CFLN) was created as a merging of the London-based Comité Nationale Français (French National Committee) and Giraud's civil and military command in Algiers.

In June 1943, under the command of General Cochet who had been appointed as chief of intelligence and direct action and, as such, was responsible for the London-based and Algiers-based elements, an "F" Staff was also created. Its mission was to have the operational command over all of the Free French "F" Force based in Britain or operating in France. "F" Staff was short lived and was disbanded in December 1943 in the midst of endless administrative bickering.

Within the BCRA, the atmosphere was then understandably grim. During the second half of 1943, following the arrest of General Charles Delestraint (1879-1945)[4] and Jean Moulin (1899-1943), a former Chief of Staff of Air Minister Pierre Cot, the BCRA was at the heart of conflicts of interest. Two of Passy's deputies, Jacques Bingen and Pierre Brossolette, contributed to the bad atmosphere by their constant disagreements. The internal intrigues flourished and, at a point, even managed to discourage Passy. He then tendered his resignation to de Gaulle and requested to be posted to a combat unit. De Gaulle refused categorically, as he saw Passy as a faithful officer.

On 4 October 1943, de Gaulle imposed a cooperation agreement between the BCRA and the Algiers services grouped under the Service de Renseignement et d'Action (Intelligence and Direct Action Service or SRA in French), placed under the command of General Gabriel Cochet who immediatly did everything he could to incorporate the BCRA under his command but in vain.

Finally, de Gaulle solved the conflict by deciding a fusion of the different services. On 27 November 1943, the French Committee of National Liberation (CFLN) issued a decree on the establishment of a Direction Generale des Services Spéciaux (Directorate of Special Services or DGSS) placed under the command of Jacques Soustelle[5].

---

3. A year later, in June 1944, the CFLN became the Gouvernement Provisoire de la République Française (Provisional Government of the French Republic or GPRF).
4. General Delestraint was arrested 9 June 1943, by Gestapo agents in the La Muette metro station. He was held in the Fresnes prison then was deported to the Struthof camp in July 1943. In September 1944, he was transferred to the Dachau concentration camp and was shot on 19 April, 1945. He was posthumously. made a Compagnion de la Liberation. He held the following decorations: commander of the légion d'honneur, Croix de Guerre 1914-1918 and 1939-1945 and Belgian Croix de Guerre.
5. The DGSS was then composed of a technical directorate (DTSS), a documentation and research center, a technical control directorate and a Joint Services Security directorate.

Claude Lamirault a.k.a "Fitzroy or "Roy"

Born in Paris on 12 June 1918, Claude Lamirault was the son of a lawyer. After having studied in the best schools in Paris he became a disciple of the thinker Charles Mauras and joined the far right Action française party.

Between 1936 and 1938, he did his military service in the 27th Mountain Rifles Battalion (27th BCA). He also served with the same battalion when he was mobilized in September 1939. He met among its members many men who would soon join the Jade Fitzroy network. He was appointed to the intelligence office of the French forces operating in Belgium as a liaison officer to the Intelligence Service. After the defeat, he decided to reach England through North Africa. He arrived in London in October 1940 and joined to the FFL in late 1940. There, he met Honoré d'Estienne d'Orves.

Lamirault was parachuted in the region of Rambouillet on behalf of the MI6 as early as December 1940. The British services had realized he was a highly motivated individual.

He had been given nearly 50,000 francs in order to build an extensive network in both the occupied and the non-occupied zones areas, with the aim of gathering military intelligence. He did not hesitate to recruit agents within his own family, including his wife, Denise, called "La Panthère", his brother (who died in captivity at the age of 17), and his closest friends, including veterans of the 27th BCA. His wife, despite her children, accepted to do this dangerous work with him. Their joint action continued until 1944.

The end result of the December 1940 mission was the creation of the Fitzroy Jade network. Among his closest agents were Pierre Hentic a.k.a "Maho", Eugene Perrot the radio operator, and a Russian intelligence expert named Kilesso

From the end of 1942, he managed to bring together agents from all sides of the political spectrum in nine subnetworks.

The Jade Fitzroy network members provided intelligence reports on the activities and movements of occupation troops, but also paid close attention to the German Air Force and to aircraft production in supportof the enemy. In addition, the network conducted surveys coastal defenses.

Lamirault's network was the first to reveal the construction of secret weapons (V1 and V2) as well as their locations.

Lamirault was parachuted no less than five times in France, despite the increasing pressure from the Germans who were desperate to neutralize him: November 1941, April, July and September 1942. In February 1943, he returned to London after a pick-up operation conducted in the region of Macon.

In March 1943, he was again parachuted into France. In August 1943, the network was the victim of an infiltration operation by the Abwehr, through an agent named Ort who was eliminated. Claude Lamirault himself was arrested on December 15, 1943 in the Richelieu-Drouot station of the Paris Metro. He managed to escape but was caught again and imprisoned at the Fresnes prison. Falling into the hands of a Catholic German intelligence officer who was the former head of a German intelligence network in the United States and who respected his opponent, he escaped torture. Meanwhile, his wife managed the network until she also was arrested in April 1944. From August 1944, the network was placed under BCRA's authority via the Alliance network.

In order to save one of his photographers called Gennetier from being arrested, Claude Lamirault may have bartered a deal based on the disclosure of the identities of two double agents. In mid-May 1944, he was transferred to Compiègne and deported to Dachau on June 5, 1944, from where he returned April 14, 1945. He then returned to the secret services with the rank of Lieutenant colonel. He died in a - mysterious - car accident on May 27, 1945, at Orleans, while serving with the military intelligence's Deuxième Bureau.

Claude Lamirault held the cross of Chevalier de la Légion d'Honneur, was a Compagnon de la Libération (Decree of 31 May 1945) and held the Croix de Guerre 1939-1945 with palm.

Between December 1940 and September 1944, the Jade Fitzroy network, fielded a total of 708 agents including 99 women.

British and Allied paratroopers about to make a descent from a Whitley on one of Ringway's dropping zones in 1941.
(RAF picture)

Henri Honoré D'Estienne d'Orves *a.k.a "Jean-Pierre"*

Born on 5 June 1901 in Verrières-le-Buisson, Henri Honoré d'Estienne d'Orves was the cousin of famous writer and pilot Antoine de Saint-Exupéry. At the age of 20, he entered the prestigious Ecole Polytechnique. Graduating in 1922, he then chose to join the Marine nationale (French Navy). Promoted to the rank of Enseigne de vaisseau de 1re classe (Navy sub-Lieutenant) in December 1925, he then followed the normal career path of a French naval officer of those times, alternating position in the Far East, in France and on board different cruisers. In 1937, he graduated from the Ecole de guerre navale and Centre des hautes études navales (French Naval War College). When war broke out, d'Estienne d'Orves was posted to Egypt, in Alexandria as deputy to the chief of staff of Force X under the command of Admiral Godfroy on board the cruiser Duquesne, with the rank of Lieutenant de vaisseau (Navy Lieutenant). On learning of the fall of France and remaining true to his Catholic and monarchist family values, he decided to reach London where he arrived in September 1940. On arrival, he was appointed to the 2e Bureau of the Free French Naval Forces (FNFL) staff and was placed in charge of intelligence gathering missions and promoted to the rank of capitaine de corvette (Lieutenant Commander). Wanting a piece of the action, he volunteered for missions inside France; he then was posted to the BCRA.

On 22 December 1940, he landed in Plogoff, Brittany, from the Marie-Louise, a Breton fishing boat. With him came his radio operator, an Alsatian by the name of Alfred Gaessler who would soon betray him. D'Estienne d'Orves' mission was to create an intelligence gathering network, which would be called Nemrod, and which would cover the West of France. Settling in the city of Nantes, d'Estienne d'Orves travelled often, both in the West of the country and to Paris. On 20 January 1941, the Gestapo arrested him in his home in Nantes. Following the informations provided by "Marty", his radio operator, the whole network was soon dismantled and its members arrested.

Henri Honoré d'Estienne d'Orves was subjected to harsh detention measures; for more than seven months, he was brutally interrogated, first in Brest, then, from the end of January, in Berlin, before being held in the Cherche-Midi prison in Paris. He is said to have nevertheless kept his charisma and good nature in spite of the rigours of his detention. His trial took place in May 1941 in front of the German martial court in Paris and lasted four days. Along with eight other members of his network, he was sentenced to death even though d'Estienne d'Orves did all he could to present himself as the ringleader and sole culprit. The president of the tribunal, along with French Admiral Darlan asked d'Estienne d'Orves and his two main deputies Maurice Barlier and Yan Doornik to be pardoned; the prospect of the pardon was promising until the 21 august 1941 and the assassination of a German officer in Paris by a Communist résistant.

Transferred to the Fresnes prison on 9 June 1941, the three prisoners were shot on 29 August 1941, at the Mont Valérien near Paris. They had refused to be blindfolded. Because of his morale strength and personality, d'Estienne d'Orves then became a symbol for the Résistance and was soon known as the "first martyr of Free France".

Henri d'Estienne d'Orves was posthumously promoted to capitaine de frégate (Navy Commander) and awarded the cross of the Libération.

Left.
On 22 December 1940, Lieutenant de vaisseau Honoré d'Estienne d'Orves landed from a sailing boat near Plogoff. He was the first emissary of the French secret services to have been equipped with a radio transmitter. He later was betrayed by his radio operator and became the first Free French to be shot by German firing squad.
(Musée de l'Ordre de la Libération picture)

The DGSS absorbed the Free French Special Services, namely the SAR and the BCRA; the latter still retained its autonomy. The DGSS was placed under the control of the COMIDAC (Comité militaire d'action en France). Giraudist and Gaullist agents merged their administrative services, in favor of better coordination of intelligence gathering, operations and counterintelligence activities. In addition, a technical directorate was added. From 2 December 1943, Passy, as a Soustelle's assistant, was tasked with the coordination of intelligence gathering, direct action and counterintelligence missions. But in his new role, Passy conflicted with François d'Astier de La Vigerie, who meanwhile had become the military delegate of the military operation Committee in France, which had been established in February 1944; Passy did not appreciate the creation of this structure. The disagreements between d'Astier de La Vigerie and Passy, which grew ever stronger from their meeting in April 1942[6] on even transpired on the operations, which did not always take into account the guidelines of the Comité d'action (Operations Committee) in France.

Thus, in spite of the unifying effort, the Giraudists and Gaullist secret services suffered from the antagonisms of their respective leaders. In addition, the psyche of the BCRA men, young and open to new methods, was very different to the habits of the more traditional or even archaic Vichy intelligence experts. In Algiers, the situation remained difficult because Giraud continued to rely on the anti-Gaullists. Within the DGSS, the counterintelligence service remained the prerogative of the former members of the Vichy military intelligence service.

Despite numerous meetings, especially in London, the success of the merging of the intelligence services was not guaranteed. Giraud himself was very critical of the BCRA's attempt, through Passy, to create a radio cell in Algiers and to recruit volunteers for missions in France. Passy believed that the secret services had to be attached to de Gaulle in his role as head of the government. He believed that high-grade intelligence should only be disseminated to the FFL while only the intelligence relating to the preparation of the landings in Europe should be communicated to the

6. Passy, who tended to be quite sectarian hated François d'Astier de La Vigerie who, to him, displayed the mind of an aristocratic and cynical adventurer.

Top.
On 11 August 1944, on Harrington air base, in the United Kingdom, members of the "Anis" mission, including Cécile Pichard in the center of the picture, have just donned their equipment and are about to board an american aircraft. (National Archives picture)

Bottom.
A German bilboard publicizing the execution of a Frenchman accused of spying activities (François de Rochenoire collection picture)

Top.
In mid-January 1944, Emmanuel d'Astier, who was the commissary of the Comité Français de la Libération Nationale (CFLN) managed to persuade Winston Churchill to provide more weapons to the Résistance. Two months later, the BCRA estimated that 35 to 40,000 men had been armed in France.
(Musée de la Résistance des Alpes-Maritimes picture)

Left.
Wiring diagram drawn by the Sicherheitsdienst (SD) in March 1943. It was based on captured documents and on agent and Résistance fighters interrogations. At that specific time, the Germans considered the Armée Secrète (AS) as the most dangerous Résistance organization inside occupied France. The AS became the primary target of the German services.
(Jean-Pierre Dramont collection)

Allies[7]. In contrast, the ex-agents of the intelligence service of Vichy[8] were in favor of sharing data with the United States and strived for the services to be attached to the staff of the FFL.

The DGSS was split in two services: the London-based Bureau de Renseignement et d'Action de Londres (the Intelligence and Direct Action Bureau of London or BRAL) headed by André Manuel, and the Algiers-based Bureau de Renseignement et d'Action

---

7. During the Casablanca Conference (13 to 24 January 1943) the Allies decided on a landing on the French West coast in spring 1944. The position of COSSAC (Chief of Staff to the Supreme Allied Commander) was created in April 1943; he was in charge of dealing with all the problems related to the preparation of the landing. In December 1943, the COSSAC became the SHAEF. The landing dates and details were set during the Cairo and Tehran conferences, between late November and early December 1943.

8. General Giraud worked closely with Colonel (soon to be promoted to General) Ronin, a former head of the Vichy SR. Ronin, with Giraud, employed an intelligence (SR) and a counterintelligence and military security (CD-SM) service placed under the command of Major Paillole.

Raymond Fassin a.k.a "Sif", "Piquier"

Born in Gennevilliers, Raymond Fassin was a teacher by training. He served with the 37th RIF (régiment d'infanterie de forteresse - fortress infantry regiment) in September 1935 and joined the National School of Saint-Maixent for training as a reserve officer. He was then assigned to the 4th RI (infantry regiment) with the rank of Lieutenant. In September 1939, he was posted to the Maginot Line, with the 132nd RI. Early 1940, he was sent to the Tours airbase to be trained as an aerial observer. He took the opportunity to get his pilot's license in June 1940.

Refusing the armistice, he decided to go to England. He managed to reach St-Jean-de-Luz where he embarked on a Polish ship the John Sobieski on 21 June 1940. Two days later, he enroled as a Lieutenant observer in the Free French Air Force of (FAFL) and was sent to the Franco-Belgian pilot school, located on the RAF base at Odiham (Hampshire).

In January 1941, he was assigned to the Free French Air staff and trained as a covert agent on the RAF base at Ringway, near Manchester. He excelled during training and André Dewavrin recruited him on 20 September 1940, and sent him to the BCRA.

Raymond Fassin is known for his collaboration with Jean Moulin whom he had met in the BCRA. Jean Moulin had personally chosen Fassin, as he had done for Hervé Monjaret for their parachute insertion of 2 January 1942, over Provence (Alpilles), near Eygalières.

At the end of 1942, Jean Moulin tasked Raymond Fassin with the coordination of the six regions of the three zones: East, Central and South. Fassin held the position of National Chief of the Bureau of air and sea operations (BOAM / SOAM) which then became the Operations Centre for parachute drops and landing (COPA). In early 1943, Fassin's cover was considered as blown. On the night of 17 to 18 June 1943, he was exfiltrated during a pick-up operation and returned to London.

However, at the request of General de Gaulle, he returned to France for a new mission, as a regional military delegate (mission Piquier). He then took the codename of "Barsac" and "Comet". He was parachuted during the night of 15 to 16 September 1943 in order to coordinate the paramilitary action of the resistance in the North of France (region "A" - Amiens).

One of his liaison agent betrayed him and he was arrested by the Gestapo on 2 April 1944 in Paris with his wife Henriette Gilles ("Sif 5" or "Solange" or "Carolle"). They were both imprisoned in Fresnes before being transferred on 2 May 1944, to the Loos-les-Lille prison. On 1 September 1944, Fassin was deported to the Sachsenhausen-Oranienburg camp where he arrived on 5 September. At the end of October 1944, he was transferred to Neuengamme, near Hamburg. He finally died of ill treatments and illness on 12 February 1945 in the satellite camp of Watenstedt 1 / Hermann Goering plants.

He was awarded of the Croix de Guerre 1939-1945, the Legion d'Honneur and the British King's medal.

(the Intelligence and Direct Action Bureau of Algiers or BRAA) placed under the command of André Pelabon (1910-1984). He had joined the BCRA in 1942, coming from Morocco where he was serving in the Vichy Navy and, from March 1943, was responsible for the BCRA cell in Algiers.

The BRAL planned the operations given to the French Forces of the Interior (FFI). For detailed planning, the DGSS developed a special section called "Bloc Planning" within the BRAL. This cell was placed under the command of Colonel Edmond Combaux, a Polytechnique graduate[9] (class X1924). The BRAL was reorganized in December 1943 in order to emphasis the centralization of intelligence[10]. The Direct Action Service was once again changed and expanded, with two internal branches: Planning, responsible for mission preparations and the support of Allied forces by Résistance movements during and after D-day[11], and the Bloc Opérationnel (operational block or BO) tasked with the missions per se. The Planning branch

was placed under the command of Colonel Combaux of the Deuxième Bureau (intelligence), Captain Brisac of the Troisième Bureau (operations) and Captain Miksche[12].

Throughout 1943 and with a quiet determination, General de Gaulle managed to reduce Giraud's influence. On 9 November 1943, Giraud was excluded from the

---

9. Edmond Combaux joined the FFL in London in April 1943. However, before this period, Combaux worked with different Résistance networks in occupied France, in conjunction with members of the Vichy Intelligence Service. Thus, he was in contact with the network of Robert Keller. Keller was an engineer, who, in 1942 and for nearly five months, with Pierre Guillou and Laurent Matheron, tapped German communications, via the cable connecting Paris to Metz,. The intelligence they gathered was then transmitted to the Intelligence Service. Those three Résistance fighters were finally exposed, arrested in late 1942 and deported in January 1943.

10. The BRAL has a command section and four sub-units, dealing respectively with administration (Section EM / S and general finances). As usual, the Command Section directly managed the clerks, mail, Foreign Liaisons and the Encoding Section.

11. These planned mission were supervised and approved by the dclegate of the Action Committee in France, namely General d'Astier de La Vigerie.

12. On 24 April 1944, a purely military Staff was formed within the BCRA, which was responsible for the fusion of the Planning and Operation Sections. On 6 May 1944 this EM (Etat-Major, or Staff) became the General Staff of the French Forces of the Interior (EMFFI) placed under the command of Colonel "Vernon".

Louis René de la Tousche
a.k.a "Richard Thouville"

Louis René de la Tousche, was born on 27 March 1919. He joined the Algiers-based BCRA in March 1944 from the 6e Régiment de tirailleurs algériens (6 Algerian Rifles Regiment). A regular commission Lieutenant, he was posted to the London-based BCRA on 1 July 1944 with a group of other officers such as Paul Carron de la Carrière and Henri Giese in order to go through parachute and specialised training. Under the alias of "Richard Thouville", he was parachuted in the Haute-Vienne département on 17 August 1944 within the frame of a Jedburgh mission. Promoted to the rank of Captain, he mentored Maquis with the rest of his Alexander team. Alexander was made up of three members: Louis de la Tousche and two american servicemen, Captain Stewart Alsop and Seargent Norman Franklin, the team radio operator. Team Alexander had a very successful mission, playing a key role in the liberation of the city of Angoulême on 31 August 1944. His mission was completed on 30 September 1944; at this date, he was posted to the groupement RAC Dordogne-Nord which then became the *50e Régiment d'infanterie* (50 Infantry Regiment). This unit was in particular committed to the combat operations that led to the liberation of the Royan pocket on the Atlantic coast.

(Family de la Tousche pictures)

CFLN, as was General Georges, and he saw his responsibilities limited to the role of Commander in Chief. Thus, Giraud had lost his influence and then was criticized for the support he gave to Pétain's Minister of the Interior, Pierre Pucheu, who had had belatedly decided to change side. Giraud allowed Pucheu's his visit to North Africa and his entry into Moroccan territory, via Casablanca in May 1943. Giraud changed attitude a few days after his arrival and placed Pucheu under house arrest. Then, Pierre Pucheu became the target of Communist Résistants because of his previous actions in occupied France [13]. In the fall of 1943, de Gaulle also criticized Giraud for having, from September 1943, supported the Communist Résistance movements in Corsica with the delivery of weapons and ammunition; this action was seen as an obstacle to the unification of Résistance movements then advocated by de Gaulle.

Month after month, the intrigues and tensions persisted. Giraud, who still was a member of the Comité d'action (Action Committee) and Emmanuel d'Astier de La Vigerie, the Commissaire National à l'Intérieur (National Commissioner of the Interior), still did not accept the autonomy of the BCRA and attacked Passy almost openly. On 8 April 1944, de Gaulle decided to offer Giraud the function of general inspector of the armed forces. He refused and finally withdrew from all military responsibility after an attempt on his life on 28 August 1944, in Mostaganem. Thus, de Gaulle managed to totally and permanently exclude Giraud and clear the way to appear as the sole and undisputed representative of the new Free French state.

The Direction de la Sécurité Militaire (Directorate for Military Security or DSM) kept its autonomy within the DGSS, as de Gaulle approved it, through Decision No. 8000. With this decision, General de Gaulle cleverly managed to place the counterintelligence services under the head of the government and no longer under the direct authority of the armed forces. In doing so, he reinforced his status as head of the government

From 15 April 1944, the London and Algiers-based intelligence services changed name and became the BCRAA. At the end of April 1944, a reorganization of the high command of the French forces was recommended. The existence of two private staffs was pointed out; one was intended for the French military, the other in support of the FFI and in charge of administrative

---

13. His involvement in the judgments of the Communist Resistants through the special sections he created for this purpose was held against him. He was also indicted for his responsibility in the execution, by the Germans, of French hostages chosen among Communist militants, including the 27 hostages of Camp de Choiseul in Chateaubriand on 22 October, 1941. Pucheu was sentenced to death by a military court on 4 March 1944 and shot on 20 March 1944 as de Gaulle refused to pardon him for reasons of state.

liaisons (EMFILA) under the orders of Passy[14]. Passy was appointed to this position because of the strong tensions with François d'Astier de La Vigerie, the military delegate for the COMIDAC. The special services infightings ended in May 1944, with the intense preparation for the Normandy landings.

From that period on and in spite of the special attention given to its operational capabilities during the previous years, the BCRA then only focused on its intelligence gathering missions.

In June 1944, it appeared that is was necessary to create, within the BCRAL, a Joint staff linking the F and RF Sections to the Staff of the French Forces of the Interior (EMFFI); this staff was in turn controled by three officers: Colonel "Vernon," Lieutenant Colonel Buckmaster for the British side and Lieutenant Colonel Van der Stricht for the U.S. Army. Eventually, under the direct leadership of the Supreme Command of the Allied Expeditionary Forces (Supreme Headquarters Allied Expeditionary Forces - SHAEF), the EMFFI ended up being solely composed of French officers with a few seconded British or American officers. The EMFFI remained operational until 23 September 1944, until the covert actions were considered as finished. After a phase designed to tie up all loose ends, the EMFFI was officially disbanded on 1 December 1944.

DE GAULLE'S DESIRE TO CONTROL THE RÉSISTANCE MOVEMENTS.

Gradually, de Gaulle realized he needed to harmonize and rationalize the organization of the French forces into a more concentric format. The full involvement of Jean Moulin allowed the establishment of a Conseil National de la Résistance (National Council of the Résistance or CNR) to unite all the political tendencies of the French Résistance. The goal was to avoid political tensions and differences between the Résistance within occupied France and the FFL.

General de Gaulle and the BCRA did not accept the existence, in Switzerland, of a delegation from the "Combat" network, which was Communist and escaped Gaullist control. It was directly sending to London intelligence destined to the Americans[15]. This came at the worst possible time for de Gaulle who was then trying to impose himself to the Americans as the only leader of the Free French at the expense of Giraud. In addition, de Gaulle's Secret Services had found out that the Americans were able to send a cable from London to Lyon to members of the "Combat" network in an average of eight days while it would normally take ten days through BCRA agents[16]. The "Combat" network, which was under the command of Pierre Frenay exerted quite an influence on the Mouvements Unis de la Résistance (United

Movements of the Résistance or MUR); this convinced de Gaulle he had to unify the Résistance movements through Jean Moulin.

In this context, Passy, Brossolette and a British agent called Yeo

14. Internally, the EMFILA was based on two structures: the BCRAL in charge of the organization and operational use of the military Résistance inside France, and the MMLA (Mission militaire de liaison administrative - Military Mission for administrative liaison) to liaise with the Allied High Command on issues pertaining to operational planning in preparation for D-day.
15. *Combat* sent military, technical, economic and political Intelligence to the U.S. services.
16. Robert Belot, Gilbert Karpman, *op. cit.*, page 296.

Top.
Major Paul Paillole MBE, head of the German section of the contre-espionnage (CE or counterintelligence) from 1935 to 1937, then deputy chief of the CE (1937-1940), head of the clandestine CE and finally head of the Sécurité militaire (1940-1944).

Top.
On 6 May 1944, in the courtyard of the direction de la Sécurité militaire in the El Biar district of Algiers, General Louis Rivet gives his last military salute. Left to right, Colonel André Serot, Colonel du Crest de Villeneuve (head of SR Terre), General Louis Rivet and Major Paul Paillole.
(Archives Paillole picture)

Joël Le Tac

Joël Le Tac was born in Paris, where, after his primary studies, he obtained a Law degree. The armistice found him as an infantry cadet officer; he refused to admit the defeat of France and managed to reach England. He then joined the Free French Forces and became a Sergeant; in October 1940, he joined the *1re compagnie d'infanterie de l'air* (1st Air Infantry Company) under the command of Captain Bergé. He gained his para wings in December 1940 and, after several months of intense preparation on March 15, 1942, he participated in Operation Savanna in the vicinity of Vannes. Because of an incomplete intelligence picture of the enemey situation, the operation was a partial failure. Unlike the rest of the team, Joël Le Tac remained in France and operated with the Résistance in the occupied zone, with the help of his brother Yves.

He then joined another direct action team, which was, in May 1941, tasked with the destruction of the Pessac power plant in the Gironde département as part of Operation Josephine B.

In August 1941, after having established contacts with Résistance movements in the non-occupied area such as Georges Bidault and Pierre Bertaux, he returned to England, through Spain.

He returned to Brittany during the night of October 13 to 14, 1941, this time as a Second Lieutenant. He helped establish the Overcloud network which was considered as one of the leading direct action network in the occupied zone, organizing weapons and equipment airdrops as early as the end of 1941. Joël Le Tac even used the house of his parents in Saint Pau, near Brest as a rendez-vous point for the exfiltration of resistants and agents to the British Isles.

After a quick return trip to the UK in January 1942, he returned to France to conduct sabotage missions but the network was soon to be almost completely destroyed. Joël Le Tac himself was arrested on February 5, 1942 in Rennes by the German military police.

Just like his family, he was deported but they all managed to return safely to France at the end of the conflict. Joël Le Tac, however almost died on several occasions: in the Struthof camp (Alsace) where he was transferred in September 1944, in Dachau and in Neuengamme in October 1944, and finally in Gross-Rosen (Silesia). In January 1945, he was transfered by train from this camp before the arrival of the Soviet army; he was the only survivor of his car, which contained over a hun-

dred deportees. He then worked in the Dora camp before being transferred to Bergen-Belsen. He finally was liberated by British troops on 15 April 1945. He was soon reinstated within the special services of General de Gaulle, and more specifically in the Direction Generale des Etudes et Recherches (Directorate of Studies and Research or DGER).

In addition to a civilian career in cosmetics, textiles and food sales, Joël Le Tac also served in Korea, as an intelligence officer and then as a company commander in the French battalion of the United Nations forces in Korea between January 1952 and 1953.

Subsequently, he worked as a journalist, freelance writer and reporter, before becoming a member of the Paris Match magazine editing board.

Top.
On 15 March 1941, during an SOE/BCRA mission, Joël Le Tac MM (in the middle, surrounded by british sailors) gets ready to launch canoes from an RAF motorboat in order to link up with his radio operator Alain de Kergolay in the aber Benoît river, near Saint-Pabu.
(Jean-Louïs Le Bihon collection)

Top.
An ID picture of Joël Le Tac after his arrest taken rue des Saussaies in 1942, by the Sicherheistdienst (SD) biometry services.
(Archives de la Police picture)

Thomas who was taken in as an observer, travelled to France, from February to April 1943, to in order to get a clear picture before any decision was taken by General de Gaulle.

They made contact with five Résistance movements in the former North Zone[17] in order to form the basis of a secret army, whose direction was given to General Delestraint (code name "Vidal"). They also gathered the opinions of various unions and of six political parties on their views about the possibility of creating the CNR. The three agents' agenda was to make sure the different sides of the political spectrum was ready to recognize de Gaulle as the unique leader of a new Fighting France.

In May 1943, the CNR was created and Jean Moulin became its first president. He did not last long in this new position as he was betrayed and was arrested on 21 June, 1943. However, in 1942, Moulin had managed to unify the main Résistance movements of the Southern Zone such as "Combat", "Franc-Tireur" and "Libération Sud" making thus possible the establishment of a Comité de Coordination de Zone Sud (South Zone Coordinating Committee or CCZS) which was effective as of November 1942. Jean Moulin's work also led to the creation of the Mouvements Unis de Résistance (MUR) on 26 January 1943. The three main Résistance movements of the South zone even agreed to perform a genuine integration of the paramilitary elements of the Résistance movements active in occupied France by creating the Armée Secrète (Secret Army or AS). The AS was then placed under the command of General Delestraint.

If de Gaulle wanted to legitimize his authority as the leader of Free France within the various Résistance movements operating in occupied France, including the Communist Francs-Tireurs Partisans (FTP), on the contrary from 1943 on, the French Communist Party[18] strove to strengthen its influence on the same movements and to force General de Gaulle to recognize this situation. On 23 December 1943, the FTP and the Secret Army merged but this merger did not affect the autonomy, the hierarchy or structure of the FTP, the Communist group remaining fanatically attached to its autonomy.

The relations between de Gaulle and Frenay improved after the arrest of Jean Moulin, as Frenay accepted an agreement with the BCRA "for the exchange in France and here [London] of any letters departing or emanating from agents operating in France belonging to the BCRA Executive Committee and to our delegation. Misunderstandings should disappear if this agreement is carefully applied"[19]. But the fact remained that Combat tried nevertheless to maintain its relative autonomy thanks to the Résistance cells in Switzerland, both vis-à-vis the Gaullists and the British services.

THE CREDIBILITY OF THE BCRA IN THE EYES OF THE ALLIES

General de Gaulle's secret services were largely dependent on the logistic support provided by the British services such as the Intelligence Service (IS) and the Special Operations Executive (SOE). The IS did not accept gracefully that the BCRA was also in contact with the SOE. On

Top.
General de Gaulle being presented "young French volunteers" in Brymach in Wales during the Summer of 1940. The General is in company of Captain Lescure (right) and Sergeant Joël Le Tac (left). In less than a year, Joël Le Tac would be operating for the BCRA.
(Amicale des Cadets picture)

17. According to Passy, those five movements were: Mouvement de la libération, de la résistance, de l'OCM, des Francs-Tireurs et Partisans (FTP) et Libération Nord.
18. The movements *Combat, Franc-Tireur, Front national, Libération,* and the Communist Party adopted a common position which was fundamentally hostile to Pierre Laval's decision to send young Frenchmen to Germany in exchange for French POWs. He signed a decree dated 4 September 1942, establishing that men aged 18-50 and women aged 21-35 could be requisitioned for compulsory labor service (STO - Service du travail obligatoire).
19. Telegram n°18. For Iris from Azur, signed Xaintrailles, 28 October 1943. Fonds Davet. Quoted by Robert Belot, Gilbert Karpman, *op. cit.* p. 299.

the contrary, especially between 1940 and 1941, the SOE feared that the BCRA was to act autonomously with a privileged relationship with the IS. On top of that, de Gaulle wanted to avoid at all cost that his special services were directly put under British authority... He encouraged the British to take into account the need for independence of the French services in the interest of French sovereignty. The BCRA could not be totally independent, as it had to rely on British logistic support and training centres.

At first, this resulted in a strained relationship with the Intelligence Service. Amiral Muselier himself was victim of a plot designed to destabilize the FFL. Thanks to incriminating documents that fell into British hands in January 1941, Muselier appeared as a traitor on Pétain regime's payroll. As a result, he was imprisoned. General de Gaulle, and even Passy, were skeptical about the veracity of the charges against Muselier. An investigation concluded that the documents were forged, created by the Security Chief of the French Headquarters, a man named Howard and who was working for the British counterintelligence service (MI5). De Gaulle was convinced that the whole scheme found its origin within the British Intelligence Service and

that the aim of the operation was to divide the French services and discredit the FFL.

From the summer of 1941, the co-operation with the French SOE became easier with the preparations of the landing regarded by all as the ultimate goal. However, the SOE remained the final authority for the operational missions that it could cancel or approve and support. Air assets were limited because the allied secret services could only rely on two squadrons to carry out covert actions across Europe. These were 136 and 137 Squadron, with a total of 33 aircrafts: Halifax, a few Hudson, Whitley (mostly used for agents training) and a dozen Lysander. The asset's limitations contributed to tensions between the IS - considered a priority - the SOE, and even the BCRA since the IS sometimes doubted the value of the operations the BCRA wanted to conduct. Thus, for the IS, exfiltrating personalities of the Résistance from occupied France was not a priority as it was for the BCRA from the spring of 1942. During this same year, the tensions between the BCRA and the SOE flared up when the political issue of military operations in France was brought up.

There were even a few sensational hiccups that exposed the bureaucratic inertia of the London-based services. Members of the Confrérie Notre-Dame (CND) network, originally established by "Rémy" in September 1940, suffered from a sloppy treatment of the intelligence reports they sent. Indeed, in 1941 and in 1942, they spent months gathering intelligence on the movements of the three heavy cruisers Scharnhorst, Gneisenau and Prinz Eugen. In February 1942, they warned London that the vessels were leaving Brest and were heading towards the German coasts, providing a unique opportunity for the British to attack them in the Channel. However, the intelligence report of their imminent departure from Brittany was discounted in London and the three ships managed to safely reach their destination.

On the other hand, other intelligence reports that had been quickly obtained by members of the CND benefited from a very quick "treatment", which was a guarantee of

Daniel Cordier
a.k.a "Alain", "Benjamin", "Michel", "Talleyand", "Toussaint" ou "BIP W" "BX10"

Daniel Cordier was born on 10 August 1920 in a conservative Catholic family in the city of Bordeaux. He joined the royalist Action française political group at the end of his teens. When the Armistice of June 1940 was signed, he was a month away from being called for active service. He immediatly decided to reach French North Africa with a few comrades from the cercle Charles Maurras he had created in Bordeaux. The ship they boarded in Bayonne ended up instead in Falsmouth on 25 June 1940. After the mandatory security checks in London, he was posted to the newly created Bataillon de Chasseurs des Forces françaises libres.

As a new recruit, he followed various courses in Delville Camp, Camberley and Old Dean. After a few weeks, the new battalion was not considered a viable unit so its members were posted to different units. Cordier then followed an officer's course and was promoted to the rank of aspirant (Cornet) in August 1941. His hopes of seeing action in North Africa being once again quashed, he decided instead to join the BCRA. He then had to follow another year of training in different techniques, tactics and procedures including sabotage, communication, security measures, clandestine landing and parachute operations etc.

Daniel Cordier was given the alias "Bip W" and carried out his first mission in occupied France in the Montluçon region where he was parachuted on 26 July 1942. His task was to be the personal assistant and radio operator of Georges Bidault, the head of the Bureau d'Information et de Presse (the clandestine Information and Press Bureau).

He met Jean Moulin in Lyon at the beginning of August 1942. Jean Moulin was very appreciative of Daniel Cordier's work and decided to have him work directly for him as head of his clandestine staff and as his own private secretary.

Cordier's influence soon spread and by the Spring of 1943, he also was active in the North zone. When Jean Moulin was arrested, Cordier kept his key position as the secretary of the Délégation Generale en France with Claude Bouchinet-Serreulles, the official successor of Jean Moulin.

In March 1944, Gestapo pressure being at its highest, Cordier returned to the United Kingdom through Spain where he spent some time in the Miranda camp. By the end of May, he was in London and was placed in command of the BCRA's agent drops section. He kept this position until the BCRA became the Direction Generale des Etudes et Recherches (DGER).

From the Autumn of 1944, Cordier became Passy's personal assistant while at the same time managing the BCRA archives in cooperation with Stéphane Hessel. He was made a Compagnon de la Libération by a 20 November 1944 decree. He then resigned from the DGER in January 1946 as Charles de Gaulle left his position as provisional president of the French republic. In the eighties, he started writing a series of books on Jean Moulin, underlining his key role in the Résistance.

Daniel Cordier has been a member of the Coulci of the Ordre de la Libération since 2005. He was made a grand officer of the Légion d'Honneur on 13 July 2012.

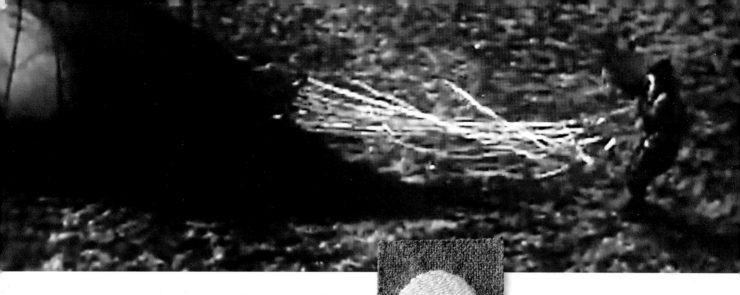

Top and Bottom.
Roughly two thousand agents were inserted inside occupied France in four years of German occupation. Of those, about half were French, the rest being British, American or Poles.
(Now it can be told document)

Top.
The "Light Bulb". This parachute qualification badge was issued to trained parachutists who were not posted to airborne units. It was worn by some SOE, BCRA and OSS agents.
(Frédéric Vernon collection)

success. Thus, Roger Dumont a.k.a "Pol", member of the BCRA and a member of the CND obtained, with the help of resistants from Le Havre, valuable intelligence on the German air detection systems located in Bruneval in the manoir de la Falaise. Thanks to a new and particularly efficient generation of radar, the Germans could now compute the altitude and distance of the aircrafts in flight. Based on the data transmitted by "Pol", Lord Louis Mountbatten, who ran the combined operations from October 1941, decided to launch an airborne operation as a naval action would have been dangerous because of the German fortifications overlooking Bruneval. In February 1942, what came to be known as Operation Biting was a great success, (see boxed text). But "Pol" was arrested shortly afterwards.

Meanwhile, the relationship between the BCRA and the U.S. Services, represented by the Coordinator of Information (COI), improved significantly. This Coordination Service of the U.S. intelligence services was established in July 1941, and placed under the orders of William Donovan. In June 1942, the COI became the Office of Strategic Services (OSS). The BCRA and the OSS had the same desire to grow in strength and importance but also the same obligation to rely on British services. This was particularly true for the Americans. The OSS started to take the BCRA seriously after the success of two important missions: first the demolition operation conducted on 26 and 27 July 1943, on the Grigny dam in order to block the transit of the German E-boats and pocket submarines through the Saone and the Rhone canals, then the double Armada mission (August-September and November-December 1943) which resulted in the destruction of the Chalon-sur-Saône power plant. During the night of 1 to 2 September 1943, the first phase of this mission targeted the power plant itself (putting it out of commission for almost six months) while the second phase targeted the power lines linking Eguzon to Paris.

Then, because of its operational results, the British SOE finally started giving more credibility to the BCRA. Since it also was in charge of subversive operations[20] in occupied territories, the SOE asked the BCRA teams to perform some missions in support of its objectives. This is how the BCRA lent its support to different plans such as the Jedburgh, Sussex and Proust[21] programs. If the Sussex plan essentially was based on intelligence missions with the dispatch in occupied France of 32 teams, the Jedburgh plan was Direct Action focused. Its purpose was to drop agents in three-man teams with the task of building the Résistance movements' capabilities in order to turn them

Right and Bottom.
Two pictures of Lieutenant Claude Bouchinet-Serreulles, one taken in London in 1941 and the other, on the left, used on a forged identity document. He had reached London in June 1940 as an interpreter, head of the personel branch and aide de camp to General de Gaulle before joining the BCRA and being sent to occupied France at the end of 1942. After Jean Moulin's arrest, he was the provisional head of the Conseil National de la Résistance (CNT). Going back to London in March 1944 in order to report on the evolution of the CNT, he was to be parachuted in France again, near Mâcon on 15 August 1944.
(Musée de l'Ordre de la Libération picture)

20. The British took an interest in subversive operations in the early 1900s, in the lights of setbacks suffered during the Boer War in South Africa. But it is particularly during the inter-war years that they got inspired by the Dutch commando model, which had caused them so much trouble in South Africa. They remodeled it and used professionals, in civilian clothes or in uniform, who specialized in targeting key nodes behind enemy lines. Subversive operations became the prerogative of the SOE which, in July 1940, reported to the Ministry of Economic Warfare. Two years before the beginning of the Second World War, the subversive operations had been recognized by the Service Military Intelligence Research (MIR) of the War Office and Section D of the Foreign Office.
21. See boxed text, p.116, 120 and 124.

Right.
SOE Type A Mk II radio suitcase. Communications between the "Confrérie Notre-Dame" network and the SR in London only started improving from August 1941 when a signals expert and four radio suitcases were parachuted into France.
(IWM picture)

into a combat force ready to conduct destruction and harasment missions in support of Allied landings.

From the Spring of 1943, the BCRA contributed to the formation of Jedburgh teams. Those teams were made up of American, British and French agents. For the French component, the BCRA provided some 108 agents, including 17 radio operators. For the Sussex and Proust programs, the BCRA respectively provided 101 agents, including two women, and 30 agents.

In mid-August 1943, according to official memos, nearly 75% of the overall intelligence on occupied France was being provided by the BCRA[22]. Between July 1943 and July 1944, the BCRA transmitted between 23% and 45% of the reports received by the OSS services in London, which represented nearly 1,5 to 4 times more than the IS[23].

From the second half of 1943, the drive and élan of the BCRA turned it into a key player between General de Gaulle's staff and the Résistance in occupied France, as well as between the FFL and the Allies. The relationship

with the British special services was apeased and the partnership between the French and British services was then considered as devoid of any ulterior motives.

However, after Jean Moulin had been arrested (in June 1943), the British services (Intelligence Service and SOE) put pressure on the BCRA for it to promote the decentralization and the fragmentation of the resistance networks in France. In answer to that request, "Passy" divided France into 12 regions, six in the formerly called North Zone and another six in the South. Each region received a Délégué Militaire de Région (area military delegate or DMR). The DMRs were coming from diverse social backgrounds and were trained in England on covert operations. Their mission was to ensure the proper execution of the military plans devised and transmitted by the BCRA. Given their responsibilities and their knowledge of codes and procedures, each of those agents carried a cyanide pill, just like their operational counterparts tasked with direct action missions. As they were very exposed, their task was dangerous and they could not run the risk of disclosing any information if captured. By the end of January 1944, five of the twelve DMRs had already been arrested or were dead (like Lieutenant Colonel Pierre Marchal, a.k.a "Morinaud" or "Moreau", DMR coordinator, who chose to swallow his cyanide pill).

In fact, the results achieved by the DMRs depended on their ability to agree with each other and to impose themselves on the local Résistance movements' leaders; it was often a matter of credibility, personal charisma and legitimacy. The DMRs also had to take into account the autonomist character of the FTP as well as the parallel actions being carried out by the Organisation de Résistance de l'Armée (Organization of the Armed Forces Résistance or ORA), which had been created on 31 January 1943, in the South Zone, and was Giraudist by tradition. However, from the Summer of 1943, the ORA recognized the authority of Charles de Gaulle.

Then, on 23 December 1943, the FTP and the Secret Army[24] signed an agreement on joint action. Finally, in February 1944, a Comité d'Action Militaire de la Résistance (Military Action Resistance committee or COMIDAC and then COMAC) was set up to in order to improve the relationships between the French services in London, the DMR and civilian authorities[25]. The Regional Military Delegates were also responsible for liaising between the BCRA and the different French regions: the regions were designated from R1 to R6 for the South, and A, B, C, D, M and P for the North[26].

Thus, the establishment and the operation of the BCRA took place in a complex time marked by political power struggles. This environment certainly deprived the BCRA of some of its operational agility. Nevertheless, the French services carried out more and more missions as the war went on, particularly in 1943 and 1944.

Marguerite Petitjean
a.k.a "Michelle Pradier", Emma", "Binette"

Marguerite Petitjean was born on 24 October 1920 in Strasbourg. Refusing to accept the defeat of France in 1940, she was thrown in jail twice for the distribution of leaflets advocating résistance to the Germans. She then decided to head for French North Africa and landed in Morocco in April 1942. There, she joined the Air Force's social services. Her commander, Major Pélabon, put her in contact with local Gaullist movements. After the Allied landings in North Africa of November 1942, she linked up with Pélabon in Algiers; meanwhile, he had become the head of the BCRA office in North Africa. In September 1943, she left Algiers and reached London; a month later, having volunteered for missions inside occupied France, she started training as an "action" agent. During the night of 29 to 30 January 1944, she was parachuted over DZ "Ajusteur" in Saint Uze near Tain-L'Hermitage in the Drôme département. Yvon Morandat OBE a.k.a "Arnolphe" who was tasked with establishing liaisons with political parties and trade unions, René Obadia a.k.a "Pioche", a saboteur, and Eugène Déchelette DSO a.k.a "Ellipse" the R5 DMR in charge of the Corrèze, Indre, Haute-Vienne and Dordogne départements jumped with her. Once in Lyon, Marguerite Petitjean operated as a liaison agent between her commander Louis Burdet a.k.a "Circonférence", Pierre Fourcaud DSO, OBE a.k.a "Sphère", Bourges-Maunoury DSO and Gaillard a.k.a "Triangle" the SAP deputy of Camille Rayon a.k.a "Archiduc".

On 3 August 1944, Marguerite Petitjean left France thanks to a pick-up operation; she reached London via Corsica and Algiers. A month later, "Binette" was promoted to the civil service rank of chargé de mission de 2e classe (equivalent to Lieutenant) and posted to the DGER in Paris. Decorated with the Cross of chevalier de la Légion d'Honneur at 23, she also held a Croix de Guerre with five citations and was decorated by General de Gaulle himself.

Right and bottom.
BCRA reports sent to London on the German institute located rue Saint-Dominique à Paris.
(Archives Nationales documents)

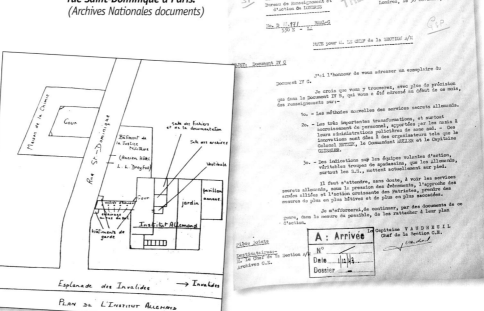

---

22. Note 3 500/D BCRA, 1 A/P dated 16 August 1943. Quoted by Guy Perrier, *Le colonel Passy et les services secrets de la France libre*. Paris, éditions Hachette Littératures, 1999, page 182.
24. Sébastien Albertelli, *op. cit*, page 360.
25. The Secret Army resulted in the combination of the *Combat* and *Franc-Tireur groups* in the Lyon region and *Libération Sud*. It was mainly focused on the southern half of France. In 1944, it evolved to include the French Forces of the Interior, the *Francs-Tireurs Partisans* and the ORA.
26. General Koenig, became commander of the military resistance in France on 6 June 1944, and, at the same time, head of the FFI, under the direction of General Eisenhower, then commander of the Allied Expeditionary Forces.
27. The South Zone had Lyon as its "HQ". It included: R1 (Lyon), R2 (Marseille), R3 (Montpellier), R4 (Toulouse), R5 (Limoges) and R6 (Clermont-Ferrand). The Northern Zone, which had Paris as its central point included region A (Lille), B (Bordeaux), C (Chalons-sur-Marne), D (Dijon), M (Le Mans) and P (Paris).

Parachute jumps on the Tatton Park dropping zone near the RAF Parachute School in Ringway. Many French agents did their parachute training there before deploying on operational missions. The early-types camouflaged canopies are of interest. *(RAF picture)*

THE BCRA MISSIONS
Combined Direct Action as a priority

Top right.
Insignia of the Free French Naval Forces (Forces Navales Françaises Libres or FNFL). As soon as the FNFL were created on 3 July, 1940, Vice-admiral Muselier, who originated from Lorraine, proposed the cross of Lorraine as the symbol of Fighting France. When the breast insignia was designed, its shape led many to call it " the coffin ".

THE MISSION OF THE BCRA was to plan operations answering political and military objectives. The purpose was primarily strategic, according to carefully delineated areas of operations. The BCRA also took into account the compartmentalization of France into three zones: the North Zone, North of the former Démarcation line which had disappeared on 11 November 1942, and the South-West and South East zones.

The covert missions were extremely important for the fighting French; in spite of the freely accepted risks, the agents did feel the rush of adrenalin as they prepared and deployed on operational missions. When reading the mémoires of some of those wartime agents, the feeling of living intensely, for an ideal, is everywhere to be found in spite of the permanent changes, postponments, orders, failures and tragedies. Only a strong dedication and the

capability to adapt to often-changing circumstances, backed by solid administrative, training and support structures could see the agents through the rigours of their missions.

Given the close relationship with the British and in spite of some of the early tensions, it made sense to share both intelligence and assets between the services.

According to Passy, as early as Autumn 1940 and beyond their contribution to intelligence gathering, the Free French also wanted to carry out guerilla warfare type of operations such as raids or to create non permanent " liberated areas ". The initial goal was mainly to disrupt the German preparations, on the French coasts, of future amphibious operations against the British Isles. With this common objective, the connection between the BCRA and the British SOE became more substantial. The first teams were deployed on French soil once volunteers of the right calibre had been identified, selected and trained.

SUMMER 1940: THE FIRST MISSIONS

According to "Passy", one of the first objectives of the missions conducted by the BCRA in occupied France focused on obtaining intelligence related to German invasion plans targeting the United Kingdom. At first, the Gaullist secret services had little interest for military intelligence but this changed quickly at the request of the British services.

At the request of Wing Commander Kenneth Cohen (1900-1984), head of the French Section of the Intelligence Service[1] who needed to obtain relevant intelligence on German planning regarding possible amphibious operations against the British Isles, Passy agreed to launch operations in both Brittany and Normandy.

Because of time constraints and instead of sending trained agents, Passy preferred to use ordinary civilians directly recruited in France by men he had sent for this very purpose. This method was somewhat controversial but there was not time for half-hearted measures and the urgency was such that verything had to be done in order to know precisely the assets the German forces were preparing to deploy for the invasion.

The pioneering role of some Polish officers who remained in France should not be ignored. They established the first intelligence network of the free zone: the Tudor network which began to operate in mid September 1940. Many intelligence officers of the Vichy army such as Major Paillole and colonels Baril, Rivet and Ronin also established contact with the Intelligence Service.

The BCRA provided volunteers who were trained in intelligence and on the coding and decoding of messages. The British provided funding for the operations and provided infiltration means, equipment and technical support. However, in spite of Free France being officially recognized by Churchill, the British Secret Services and even the American OSS continued to put pressure on Passy for the BCRA to be amalgamated with the British Intelligence Service. Passy resisted, even receiving some

Top.
A radio operator during a covert broadcast. Passy believed than by August 1943, the BCRA provided more than 70 % of intelligence related to France of all the Allied secret services (excluding MI.6 since information related to its activities were non releasable).
(François de Rochenoire collection picture)

The Gallia network

This network was established quite late, in 1943. Its creation was a joint venture between the BCRA and the United Resistance Movement (mouvements unis de la Résistance - MUR). The goal was to coordinate intelligence services of both the BCRA and the MUR, which political orientation was not hard-line Gaullist. Nevertheless, they still managed to work together.

Three agents, namely Henry Gorce-Franklin, Eugène Claudius-Petit and Albert Cohan, headed the network. Colonel Louis Gentil joined them at a latter date. It focused on military and security intelligence (the Security Service (SD) in relation with the Gestapo, the Feldpolizei units, the Abwehr, the Vichy police and the Milice). Its operations focused on the German order of battle and on a permanent updating of the intelligence picture on coastal fortification works. The intel reports were sent to London by the Electra radio station, which was under the command of Jean Fleury a.k.a "Panier". In the South Zone, the task of the Gallia network was also to oversee the creation and operation of five out of the twenty already established radio station. Most of those stations were operated by signal specialists coming from the recently disbanded Sûreté du Territoire police service, which had disappeared at the same time as the Free Zone in November 1942.

Over the months, and despite the multiple arrests that occurred in May and June 1943, the Gallia network grew to the point of being considered, in early 1944, as one of the Major networks on which the BCRA could rely. In July 1943, it incorporated two networks: The Belgian Reims-Noël and the Dupleix networks. In autumn 1943, the Gallia expanded its activities to the North Zone and contributed to the organization of the Unités de Combat et de Renseignement (combat and intelligence units or UCR). Colonel Louis Gentil also took command of the North Zone Gallia, which was named the Darius network. In the Spring of 1944, Darius was seriously weakened by numerous arrests among its members.

Gallia was also the network which had the highest number of agents in the South Zone; they numbered nearly 2,500. All were systematically recorded as BCRA members and were issued a personal number. They were very similar to military agents. For safety reasons, the network compartmentalization was pushed to the extreme; it was divided into regions, the regions being divided into sectors; operating on a need-to-know basis the agents had very little information to compromise when subjected to torture. Thus each of the seven operational regions that composed the Gallia network had its own intelligence service and they all worked independently.

The intelligence provided by Gallia was crucial to the advance of Allied forces and to the harassment of German forces after the Allied landings in Normandy and Provence.

The Gallia Network officially ceased operations on 15 September 1944

---

1. A Royal Navy officer, Kenneth Cohen was a torpedo expert during the inter-war period. In 1935, he was assigned to the Secret Intelligence Service (SIS) as a French and Russian interpreter. Quickly, he was appointed as the head the intelligence service on the European continent. He assumed a nom-de-guerre and a code name, respectively, "Kenneth Crane" and "Z-3". During the Second World War, Cohen worked on behalf of the SIS in the A5 Section focused on France. He recruited contact agents in the unoccupied zone. From the summer of 1943, he was associated to the Sussex Program and the drop of 54 teams of operators on the rear of the enemy lines in order to disrupt the German logistics and communications structures in conjunction with local Résistance networks.

The Brandy network

In 1942, Christian Martell, at the request of the BCRA, created the Brandy network which specialized in the evasion of pilots or aviation experts towards England. His brother, Maurice Martell, then headed the network until his arrest in June 1943. Although particularly exposed to German pressure, the network managed to help 4,000 RAF pilots, Fighting French and POWs, cross the demarcation line. The members of this network were tracked by the Germans or betrayed by the French as Maurice Martell was.

The Brandy network worked in synergy with other French networks such as the Burgundy network and sometimes with Belgian networks such as the Pat O'Leary network.

Raymond Basset was one of the key players of this network. In 1940, he created an active Résistance cell in the region of Châlons-sur-Marne. Basset escaped the Gestapo after his arrest in 1942 and, in June 1943, managed to return to London from Spain. Then, he joined the BCRA. During the summer 1943, he returned to France for a sabotage mission (the Armada Mission), against the Le Creusot industrial site. This mission was a success and several other successful sabotage missions followed it. During the summer of 1944, as the military delegate of the Rhone and the Loire regions and as part of the Gingembre mission, Basset directed and coordinated various operations against German columns in addition to the destruction of German trains. On 23 July, with a dozen FFI members, he managed to destroy a fuel train in the Vaugry station. This sabotage deprived the German troops located in the South of France of their most important petrol supplies. Finally, on 3 September 1944, he took control of the City Hall of Lyon, before the arrival of the 1st DFL (Free French Division).

Another agent of the Brandy network was André Jarrot (1909-2000) a.k.a "Jean Goujon", "Cotre" or "Crible" and "Pomeau", who was originally a member of the Ali network. From October 1940, he facilitated many illegal crossings of the demarcation line into the South Zone. Arrested in January 1942, he posed as a black market dealer. He was quickly released because his resistance activities could not be proven. In this context, he joined the Brandy network while still operating in collaboration with established Belgian, French and Spanish networks.

Jarrot, who also conducted sabotage operations, Basset, Pierrre Guilhemon and Maurice Martell were the key players in the Brandy network .

In total, F and RF Section of the SOE sent close to 900 agents to France independently of the covert operators deployed by Section R of the BCRA and by the SIS (MI.6).
(Now it can be told document)

unexpected support from the IS Deputy Director, Sir Claude Dansey, which in many ways helped to calm the stormy relationship between the French and the British services.

COVERT AGENTS OPERATING WITH PATRIOTS

Passy's method contrasted with the traditional rule of the British intelligence services. He did not want to only rely on specially dispatched agents who were tasked with filling questionnaires dealing specifically with British intelligence requests because the risks were too high and the time spent on answering the requests too long.

Instead, the agents sent to France were encouraged to come into contact with ordinary members of the public, preferably working in an areas considered as strategic, such as ports and rail workers. The idea was of course to establish intelligence gathering networks in all parts of the French population. The British and the French eventually agreed on this method.

The first French agent sent to France on behalf of the British services was Hubert Moreau. He spent fifteen days on an intelligence gathering mission in July 1940.

Among the first volunteers sent in support of the French services were Duclos a.k.a "Saint-Jacques", Beresnikoff a.k.a "Corvisart" and Jacques Mansion. Sent to France by sea, they carried out their missions successfully. Little by little the British forgot their initial doubts about the French modus operandi.

THE MANSION, DUCLOS-BERESNIKOFF, FOURCAUD MISSIONS...AND SAVANNA.

Jacques Mansion was the first agent who operated for the Gaullists services. At the age of 26, he inaugurated a long series of actions by performing an intelligence gathering mission on the Brittany coast between July and September 1940. Officially, he was asking for his administrative demobilization. His cover story as the average " grey man " allowed him to return to London with several maps giving an overview of the first German military installations along the coasts of Brittany

On 4 August 1940, Duclos a.k.a, "Saint-Jacques" and Beresnikoff a.k.a "Corvisart"[2] were tasked with an intelligence gathering mission on German activities and assets in the Ouistreham area. Their secondary mission was to set up an intelligence network covering the Somme, Calvados, Eure and Seine inférieure departments. Their return to London was complicated because of motor guboat sent to pick them up failed to see their light signals in a thick fog. "Corvisart" reached the " Zone Libre " (free zone) then Spain and returned to England on 18 January 1941. "Saint-Jacques" reached England in time for Christmas 1940, through Portugal

and North Africa after having created a large intelligence network.

Pierre Fourcaud, also known as "Lucas" was in charge of establishing a connection with the Zone Non Occupée (non-occupied zone or ZNO). Between September and December 1940, while in France and in opposition to Passy's directives, he made contact with various senior officials of the Vichy regime. One of those officials was Colonel Georges Groussard (1891-1980), the creator of the Vichy army intelligence services, called the Centre d'Information et d'Etudes (information and studies

(continued on page 66)

2. They were landed from a speedboat at Saint-Aubin-sur-Mer.

Top.
Lysander landing strip marking by a Résistance reception committee.
(Now it can be told document)

Bottom.
A Colt 1911A1 .45 ACP pistol, one of the most cherished weapons among French Résistance fighters and some ID documents produced in the United Kingdom and issued to agents who were parachuted or landed into occupied France.
(François de Rochenoire collection picture)

Top and Bottom.
BCRA, SOE and MI6 agents all had to
follow a parachute course in Ringway.
This course normally lasted for five
days but sometimes the parent services
recalled their pupils after only three or
four days in order to send them on a
pressing operational mission.
(RAF picture)

Agents training

The BCRA needed to get its agents trained in parachute operations, encryption techniques, weapons handling, combat shooting, demolition and booby traps, not to mention all the skills that would prove vital to survive more than just a few days in occupied territory. These skills were taught in different training centres but they all had one thing in common: the pace was relentless and the trainees needed to be able to learn very quickly as they were, for some of them, supposed to become fully operational in a matter of weeks. On average, if the selection rate of 1943 is to be taken as an example, only 5 out of the 30 candidates were selected (approximately 15%).

A BRITISH EXPERTISE:
THE FAMOUS TRAINING CENTRES

The SIS had already created a training school for special agents; Kim Philby (1912-1988), although a double agent working for both MI6 and the KGB, brought all his expertise to both the selection and the training process of that establishment.

At the end of 1940, the British had a saboteur training school in Brickendonbury Hill (Hertfordshire). It was called Station 17 or STS17 (Special Training School). Instructors were placed under the command of Section D.

Following the SIS initiative, the SOE also established its own training center called the Military Intelligence Wing (MI Wing), which was located in Arisaig (Inverness County) in the Highlands. Major Jimmy Munn headed the center. The training was divided into four successive phases. When they created that centre, the head of SOE for Western Europe, Colonel Gubbins, and Major Jimmy Munn were largely inspired by STS17 and they also relied on Philby's expertise.

Gradually, the SOE created a series of discreet training establishments called Special Training School (STS). There were four types of training centers, each comprising several schools.

For example, Inverie House (STS24a) located in the Highlands, or Inchmery House (STS38), located in Exbury, in southern England, were very well known to French volunteers (Free French paratroopers, RF Section of the SOE and BCRA); they had nicknamed it "Station 36". It was in essence the special agent's basic school where the aptitude of newly recruited volunteers was tested in order to gauge their ability to perform covert operations.

FOUR TYPES OF SCHOOLS
AND SPECIALIZED TRAINING ESTABLISHMENTS

The preliminary schools provided basic training including weapons and explosives handling, unarmed combat, land navigation and signals. Physical conditioning and fieldcraft training were a daily occurence. From 1943, the SOE replaced these schools with a Preliminary Assessment Centre in Cranleigh (Surrey), which was-known by the name of called "Winterfolf" or STS7. Subsequently,

(continued on page 64)

Top.
Howbury Hall school (STS 40) which taught, among other topics, the use of Eureka and Rebecca beacons in support of Lysander operations. The course lasted a week.
(François de Rochenoire collection picture)

Center.
Beaulieu, near Southampton, was one of the "Finishing Schools" where, from the end of 1940 to 1945, over 3,000 agents were trained.
(François de Rochenoire collection picture)

Right.
Trainee paratrooper donning their kit in front of a hangar in Ringway in 1941. The Sorbo helmet and the green jump smock had a distinct German influence.
(RAF picture)

Free French SAS doing their parachute course in Ringway on 6 April 1945. Nothing has changed since 1941 when the first Free French agents did their courses. (ECPAD picture)

it was decided that the selection and evaluation process would take place over four days not four weeks...

The paramilitary schools like STS21 and STS25c were located in different remote areas such as Arisaig and Morar (Inverness Shire County in western Scotland). The courses lasted 3 to 5 weeks and each session could accomodate up to 75 students; training focused on Commando-type operations and guerrilla warfare. Some of these schools were specialized, such as the Swordland or Moraort schools that focused on maritime operations or on the attack of surface ships. Of particular note is the famous STS51 jump school in Ringway, in the County of Manchester.

The "Finishing Schools"; there were eight of them (STS 31 to 38). They were gradually established between January 1941 and October 1942, in Beaulieu located in the New Forest, near Southampton. In total, they trained nearly 3,000 agents in covert operations, in operational security (Department A), in burglary techniques and lock openings (Department B), in intelligence (Department C), in covert propaganda techniques (rumours, blackmail, defamation leading to libel etc) – (Department D), and encryption techniques. (E Department).

Finally, some specialized training schools including sabotage and counter-sabotage (trains, rolling stock, railways, ships, industrial facilities, bridges), forged documents, assassination techniques (Aston House in the county of Hertfordshire), parachute operations and landing.

By war's end, no fewer than fifty special schools were active in the United Kingdom with nearly 1,400 instructors. Approximately 6,800 students were trained there, including 760 Americans.

Depending on the required skill and because of the wide range of available courses, the training which was delivered in those schools could qualify an agent as a radio operator, a liaison agent, a sabotage instructor, a landing and parachuting reception committee commander or even as a military delegate.

Top, left and next page bottom right.
The Ringway parachute school, which was in charge of training British Airborne Forces was also part of the SIS and SOE "paramilitary" schools. The agents spent three to five days there in order to get their parachute qualification.
(RAF pictures)

Top.
"Cat" Jacqueline Nearne MBE following a signal class. Jacqueline Nearne was parachuted on 25 January 1943 in the Brioude region under the name of Josette Norville. She operated as liaison officer of the SOE F "Stationer" network. She returned to the United Kingdom in April 1944.

Top right.
Agent "Cat" (Jacqueline Nearne) during a landing strip marking class.

Right.
During a sabotage class, several students and an instructor study on a model the vulnerable points of a locomotive.

Bottom.
"Felix" Harry Ree crossing an obstacle during the para-military course. Captain Henry Alfred Ree a.k.a "Cesar" was parachuted during the night of 14 to 15 April 1943 near Clermont-Ferrand as deputy of the SOE F Stockbroker network.
(Now it can be told documents)

centre) who also was in charge of Marshal Pétain's[3] protection groups. The other was Major Georges Loustaunau-Lacau (1894-1955), a Saint-Cyr graduate[4]. This initiative was disawowed by both Passy and de Gaulle as the two officers were fundamentally anti-Gaullist. However, Fourcaud's approach reflected the strategic as well as

(continued on page 72)

---

[3]. In June 1941, Groussard went to London to obtain, from Churchill, the signature of secret agreements with Vichy. He was arrested the following month on his return to France. Subjected to a strong pressure from Vichy's Prime Minister Laval services, he was arrested in early 1941. He managed to reach Switzerland where he gave a new impetus to a Military Intelligence network (the *Gilbert* Network) and worked in support of the Intelligence Service. He was fundamentally anti-Gaullist.

[4]. Before the war, Loustaunau-Lacau studied at the Ecole de Guerre (the War College) at the same time as Charles de Gaulle. At that time, he was close to the French royalist networks and then to the Parti Populaire Français. He took part in the battle of France in the Verdun area where he was severely wounded. Behind the facade of an intelligence officer in the Vichy army, he was the creator and director of the Alliance Résistance network. He was arrested in May 1941, but escaped and fought underground, but he was caught again in 1943 and deported to Mauthausen. After World War II, he resumed his pre-war job as a journalist and editor.

Left.
Drawing depicting sabotage operations carried out by Résistance fighters from the end of 1940 on. By the Spring of 1944, the BCRA controlled twenty large networks, ninety regional networks and had parachuted into occupied France one hundred and sixteen commanders and radio operators.
(Frédéric Vernon collection)

The Marco Polo network

This network was created and led by Lieutenant Commander Pierre Sonneville (1911-1970), a.k.a "Equilatéral" who had originaly joined the FFL submarine force in July 1940. Sonneville began covert operations during the second half of 1942.

In November 1942, he was parachuted in the Châteauroux region with the mission of setting up the Marco Polo intelligence gathering network. As a secondary task, he was to contact the naval officers he knew in the Toulon military base in order to get them to join the FFL. Initially, the network was based in the Lyon region but it quiclky spread to finally operate all over France but also in Germany, Holland and Belgium thanks to the relationships that scientists kept in spite of the war situation. This predominance of scientists within the network led it to pay particular attention to the German efforts to develop the V1 and V2 rockets, dedicating its operations to the gathering of technical and scientific intelligence. Thus, as soon as February 1944, the network was in a position to report the first successful air launch tests of the V1. The other particularity of Marco Polo was that many of its members originated from the Touraine region. The network also helped wanted or on-the-run individuals to cross the demarcation line, providing them with forged identification documents but its main task was to provide military, political and economic intelligence to the BCRA while also conducting counterintelligence and direct action operations. The counterintelligence efforts of the Béarn and Marceau networks were focused on the French members of the Gestapo (the so-called Carlingue); sensing that the German defeat was near, several of its members soon played a double game !

The Marco Polo network answered strictly to the BCRA. Its task was to expand its influence in the South Zone, while contacting the various existing resistance movements and networks to align them with the Gaullist guidelines. From the beginning of January 1943 on, the Marco Polo network sent a steady stream of intelligence reports to London. The German services eventually hunted the network down; many of its members were shot or deported. Pierre Sonneville escaped being arrested on several occasions and finally managed to return to London in April 1943. He went back to France on 5 April 1944, as the Military Delegate of the Paris region, operating with the Ajax network. After Sonneville's departure in 1943, Paul Guivante de Saint-Gast (a.k.a Adèle, Pélican, Polo) took command of the network; after his capture by the Germans, René Pellet a.k.a "Octave ", "Albatros" and "Polo" took his position; he also was captured and then shot by the Germans in July 1944, a few days before the liberation of Lyon.

Until the Liberation and in spite of heavy losses, Marco Polo kept on feeding its employers a steady stream of valuable intelligence reports. The network fielded about a thousand agents throughout its existence.

Left to right, several key players of the Marco Polo network: Pierre Sonneville OBE, René Carmille, Jacques Bergier and André Helbronner who died in Buchenwald on 14 March 1944.
(Frédéric Vernon collection)

Paul Rivière
a.k.a "Claude", "Sif bis", "Charles-Henri", "Marquis", " François", "Galvani", or "Renouard"

Originating from Montagny, Paul Rivière was a French teacher in Lyon. When he was mobilised at the age of 27 in 1939, he was posted to the Cavalry school in Saumur. In June 1940, he took part in the heroic defence of the river by the Cavalry candidate officers (the "Cadets de saumur") and was wounded on 20 June 1940. He was then evacuated to Bordeaux and Toulouse before returning to the Lyon region.

Demobilised in October 1940, he started teaching again while looking for ways of reaching London. He failed to reach the UK in early 1941 and thus joined the Combat résistance movement.

He became the representative of Combat in the Rhône-Alpes region and was tasked with recruiting, organising and propaganda (ROP). In January 1942, he met Jean Moulin and started assisting him in his efforts to unify résistance movements. More attracted by the operational aspects of his tasks, he was put in charge of the selection of landing and dropping zones. Arrested by the Vichy police on 23 June 1942 while receiving a parachute drop, Paul Rivière was jailed for four months. As soon as he was freed, he resumed his previous activities. Recognised as a reliable and dedicated field officer, he was, in 1943, made responsible for all parachute and Lysander mission in the South zone.

Paul Rivière was sent to London in June 1943 for further training. The arrest of Jean Moulin meant he had to be parachuted back into France with very little notice. On 21 July 1943, he landed on the "Vincent" DZ in Cormatin (Saône-et-Loire département) in order to take command of the South zone landing and parachute operations section (section des atterrissages et parachutages pour la Zone Sud).

He personally led 13 pick-up operations. Recalled to London in May 1944, he was once again parachuted in Saône-et-Loire on 7 June 1944 during Operation "John 87 A" on the "Metacarpe" DZ in Soulcy near the river Arroux, in the vicinity of the city of Gueugnon.

Top.
Paul Rivière OBE, MM was one of the great BCRA agents. He was parachuted twice into occupied France, in 1942 and in 1944.
(Musée de l'Ordre de la Libération pictures)

Pierre Brossolette
a.k.a "Pedro" then "Brumaire"

A graduate from the famous Ecole Normale, Pierre Brossolette was a journalist specialized in international relations. He wrote in several newspapers such as Europe Nouvelle, Quotidien, Progrès Civique, Notre Temps, Excelsior, Marianne, Terre Libre and the Populaire.

BETWEEN THE TWO WORLD WARS

During his military service, Pierre Brossolette served as a Second Lieutenant in the 5th RI (infantry regiment) located in Paris.

His political connections, including with Léon Blum, oriented him towards the Section Française de l'Internationale ouvrière (SFIO, the French Labour party). In 1930, he reached the position of Deputy of the Colonial Office Minister, Francois Pietri. Between 1936 and 1939, Blum appointed him to the national radio corporation where he was foreign policy editor. His hostility to the Munich Treaty led to his dismissal at the request of Edouard Daladier who was then Prime Minister.

On mobilization, on 23 August 1939, he was assigned as a Lieutenant in the 5th RI. He took command of a fore support company (with 2 mortars, 16 machine guns and two 25 mm guns) which was attached to the 21st Infantry

Battalion. He was promoted to Captain in March 1940 and received the Croix de Guerre thanks to his conduct during the Battle of France. In August 1940, he was demobilized but he was unable to find a teaching position because the Vichy administration refused to reinstate him owing to his political beliefs.

He then opened a bookstore (located at 89 rue de la Pompe in Paris), which, in the following years, was to serve as a cover for resistance activities.

JOINING THE RÉSISTANCE

After the French defeat and the signing of the Armistice, Brossolette was one of the first Frenchmen to be involved in resistance activities. From the beginning of 1941, with Agnès Humbert, he contributed to the establishment of the Musée de l'Homme Network. Then, in November 1941, after the disappearance of the Musée de l'Homme Network, he joined the Confrérie Notre-Dame, where he was in charge of the Press and Propaganda Section. He became the editor of the newspaper Résistance. It was during this period that he adopted the code name "Pedro".

On 1 December 1941, he joined the Free French Forces. He sent reports and messages to London and established contacts with Libération-Nord and the Organisation civile et militaire (OCM).

Despite the arrests that decimated networks, Brossolette managed to reach London on 27 April 1942, on board of a Lysander, which had taken off from the Rouen area (near Saint-Saëns). He was promoted to the rank of Major.

Parachuted in Chalon-sur-Saône in France, on the night of 3 to 4 June 1942, he established contacts with various personalities. Among the personalities he managed to rally to the Gaullist cause were André Philip (1902-1970), a member of the SFIO (one of the 80 MPs who had refused to give the full powers to Philippe Pétain on 10 July 1940) and Charles Vallin (1903-1948) member of the French Socialist Party.

His close ties with André Dewavrin - Colonel Passy - and the success of his covert missions to rally political leaders from the left and extreme left of the political spectrum to the Gaullist cause meant that he was soon appointed as co-director of the BCRA. On 1 October 1942, he was put in charge of the relationships between the BCRA and the resistance networks inside the French territory. He was made a compagnon de la Libération on 17 October 1942.

In January 1943, he led the Brumaire-Arquebuse mission (landing on the night of 26 to 27 January 1943), later joined by André Dewavrin and Yeo-Thomas. This mission, aimed at making an inventory of resources available to the North Zone resistance networks, while applying a clear separation between military action and intelligence missions. Finally, reliable leaders had to be identified in order to lay the foundations of the post-liberation French government.

Pierre Brossolette and André Dewavrin returned to London on 16 April 1943.

Brossolette then returned to his position as radio journalist and helped Maurice Schumann on the BBC between May and July 1943.

On 19 September 1943, in charge of a new mission, he inserted into occupied France on a Lysander, in the region of Angoulême. During this mission, he acted as adviser to the CFLN general delegate for Resistance, Emile Bollaert.

In November, his exfiltration flight by Lysander failed. He made it to the Audierne Bay in Brittany in order to embark on a fishing boat, the Jouet des flots, on the evening of 2 February 1943, along with Emile Bollaert.

Unfortunately, severe weather caused the sinking of the ship. Hidden in a resistant house in Plogoff the two men were finally arrested during a routine check. Both of them were first transferred to the Rennes prison on 5 February. During his interrogation cessions, on 16 March, Brossolette finally realized he had been betrayed and that the Germans knew of his true identity.

On 19 March, he was transferred to the Gestapo headquarters at 84 Avenue Foch in Paris. Tortured time and again, on 22 March, Pierre Brossolette managed to jump from a 5th storey window of the Gestapo office. He died after several hours of agony.

Pierre Brossolette's decorations included the Croix de Chevalier de la Légion d'Honneur, the Croix de Compagnon de la Liberation (Decree of 17 October 1942), the Croix de Guerre 1939-1945 with two citations and the Médaille de la Résistance with Rosette.

Previous page, Top left and right, and right.
Different pictures of Pierre Brossolette; in civilian clothes soon after his arrival, as a Lieutenant of the 5e RI in 1939, wearing a Battle Dress as a member of the FFL and in walking out uniform during a Free French meeting in London.

Top center.
French ID paper (" Carte d'identité ") dated 1942 in the name of Pierre Brossolette.

Bottom.
ID paper dated April 1943 in London in the name of Pierre Bourgat, Major in the Free French forces.
(Musée de l'Ordre de la Libération pictures)

Bruno Larat *a.k.a "Luc" or "Xavier"*

The son of a cavalry officer and veteran of the Great War, Bruno Larat graduated from law school in 1938. On 8 December 1938, he became a trainee lawyer at the Court of Appeal in Lyon. Attracted by the prospect of a military carreer, he undertook flight training in Bordeaux-Merignac but the defeat of 1940 caught him before he completed his course. Following the defeat and the signing of the armistice, he decided to go to England.

On November 1, he joined the Free French Training School in Odiham in order to be incorporated within the Free French Air Force rather than the RAF. But his failing health prevented him from becoming a pilot. From June 9, 1941, he was posted as an instructor to the Free French Air Forces (FAFL) base in Camberley.

In October 1941, he was posted to the staff of General de Gaulle and joined the Action Section of the BCRA. In his new position as a mission organizer with direct contacts with the Service des Opérations Aériennes et Maritimes (SOAM or Maritime and Air Operations Service), he met Jean Moulin. According to General Koenig, Larat had also volunteered to help organize resistance networks in France. He was parachuted into France on two occasions to carry out such missions, first in the Tours area and then near Paris region.

On his return to London, Bruno Larat became the head of the Bureau de coordination des opérations de parachutage et d'atterrissage (Office for the Coordination of Parachute and Landing Operations). During this period, he befriended Jean-Louis Cremieux-Brilhac and Fred Scamaroni.

During the first half of 1943, Captain Bruno Larat operated in France, from Lyon, as the officer responsible for the Centre d'Opérations de Parachutages et d'Atterrissages (Centre for Parachute and Landings Operations or COPA the new name of the SOAM). All types of assets were used, including Lysander and twin-engined Hudson. In addition to Résistance leaders transportation to and from the UK, Bruno Larat was also in charge of the reception of funds sent from England to finance resistance movements in France and of the printing of underground newspapers.

In June 1943, the Gestapo, after having "turned" a member of the Combat network, managed to arrest many resistance fighters in Marseille, including General Delestraint, the head of the Armée Secrète (Secret Army).

Given the urgency of the situation, Jean Moulin decided to order a covert meeting on June 21, 1943, in the office of Dr. Dugoujon, in Caluire, near Lyon. Jean Moulin, Raymond Aubrac, Lieutenant Aubry, Colonel Lacaze, André Lassagne, Lieutenant Colonel Schwartzfeld, René Hardy and Bruno Larat were all present. The Gestapo, led by Klaus Barbie, who had learnt of this meeting, captured them all. Larat was then tortured in Fort Montluc. The Germans wanted to know everything about the SOAM operations. At the end of August he was transferred to the Fresnes prison. In December 1943 he was sent to Camp Royallieu near Compiègne before being deported on January 29, 1944 to Buchenwald. In March 1944, weakened by the constant abuses he had been suffering from since 1943, he was transferred to Camp Dora. There, he was forced to dig tunnels to protect V1 and V2 factories. Exhausted, he died in the Dora camp infirmary on April 5, 1944.

Right and Bottom.
A member of a maquis holding an SOE torch while marking a landing strip.
(Now it can be told document)

Léon Yvon Morandat *a.k.a "Yvon" and "Pierrelot"*

Born in the Ain département, in Bellas, from an agricultural family with Left-leaning values, Léon Morandat did his military service with the Chasseurs alpins (Mountain Rifles). He was mobilised with the same unit in 1939 and took part in the Norway campaign including the battle of Narvik. On 1 July 1940, on his return to the UK, he joined the Free French forces. His personal qualities were spotted and his was soon posted to the BCRA in the intelligence gathering field, gaining his parachute wings in Largo and following a commando course in Hardwick.

In the autumn of 1941, he was sent to France in order to establish contact with trade unions, and résistance movements on the South zone. Within the frame of mission Outclass which was carried out in coordination with the SOE, he was parachuted in the Toulouse region in Fonsorbes, on the 6 November 1941. In order to carry out his mission, he joined the executive committee of the Libération-Sud résistance movement which he supported financially thanks to London-supplied money. Morandat soon realised that this particular movement deserved additional logistical support because of the important possition it held and drafted a memo to that effect for the SOE. On receiving it, the SOE decided to send a liaison agent to Libération-Sud in the person of Tony Brooks who arrived in July1942.

From January 1942, Morandat also was in contact with Jean Moulin. Together, they managed the funds that were destined to the résistance movements. During his talks with Jean Moulin, Léon Morandat proposed the organisation of a résistance parliament; Moulin did not follow him on this path. From the second half of 1942 on, the two men seemed to disagree on most issues so much so that Morandat was recalled to London in November 1942. Becoming a member of the Algiers-based Assemblée consultative in 1943, he only returned to France on 29 January 1944. He was parachuted in the Drôme département near Tain-L'hermitage with the task of supporting Alexandre Parodi in his role as General Delegate of the National Liberation Committee (délégué général du Comité de libération nationale).

A few months later, Morandat took an active part in the liberation of Paris (25 August 1944), recapturing in the name of the French provisional government the Hôtel Matignon (the office of the French Prime Minister) with only a woman to back him up (she would later become his wife). Léon Morandat held the following decorations: Grand Officier de la Légion d'honneur, Grand Officier de l'Ordre national du Mérite, Compagnon de la Libération (13 July 1945 decree), Croix de Guerre 1939-1945 with 3 citations, Médaille de la Résistance with rosette, Officer of the Order of the British Empire.

Top.
After an agent pick-up, a Hudson gathers speed before taking off.
(RAF picture)

Bottom.
One of the Royal Air Force motorboats used in support of SOE, SIS and BCRA operations. As an example, on 14 October 1941, during mission Latak (a mission known as Overcloud by the SOE), RAF 360 landed two BCRA agents: Joël Le Tac and Alain de Kergorlay, his radio operator.
(RAF picture)

tactical necessity of working in partnership with experts even if they were part of a regime which was deeply hated by the Free French.

Alhough betrayed by his radio operator, Sergeant Laroche who was " turned " by the Germans, Fourcaud managed to escape and return to London. He initially accused Roger Warin a.k.a "Wybot" of having been the cause of his arrest but then the tension between the two agents eased. On the contrary, they remained intense between Fourcaud and Passy, the latter having criticized Fourcaud's lack of professionalism and his relationships with Vichy. Passy opposed any further operational deployment for Fourcaud and the latter never forgave him.

Although intelligence gathering missions were the most numerous, some direct action missions were also prepared and carried out. One such example was given

by the Savanna mission, which is considered as the first direct action mission parachuted onto the French territory. It was decided in December 1940 and it was aimed at the Meucon Airfield, near Vannes (Morbihan). Meucon housed a German squadron, Kampfgeschwader 100 which was in charge of guiding the night bombing of London. Its normal operating procedure was to drop incendiary bombs in a triangular pattern in order to guide the following German bombers. At the request of the British Air Ministry, the aim was to kill 70 pilots and navigators as they were being ferried from their quarters to the airfield.

Initially, the plan was to use an explosive charge (a "road-trap" mine) with a pressure plate. At the last moment, a remote fire control device was favoured. As the SOE did not have any agents capable of carrying out such an operation at this time, it requested the support of the 1ere Compagnie d'Infanterie de l'Air (1st Free French Air Infantry Company, an airborne unit) which had then less than twenty men on strength.

The Savanna mission was decided, with the participation of a Free French team composed of five men under Captain Bergé OBE MC; he had carefully selected his four partners: Lieutenant Petit-Laurent, Sergeants Forman and Le Tac MM and Corporal Renault. But ethical dissensions between the British RAF and members of the British secret services delayed the launch of the mission. British military personnel found it hard to accept that the French team was going to operate in civilian clothing and not in uniform. Finally, the commando was dropped on the night of 14 to 15 March 1941, near Elven. On site, the team received some valuable assistance from two brothers who owned a local farm and from Elven's priest, Father Jarnot. But the attack on the convoy was not to happen. The French agents discovered that the

pilots got to the airfield in several different cars, while others were actually staying on the airfield. If the mission was aborted[5], however, it did provide many lessons for future operations and led to some valuable intelligence being gathered.

One of those lessons was that nothing significant could be achieved without the establishment of strong secondary networks capable of supporting the different actions as they were being planned and conducted in accordance with Passy and General de Gaulle's aspirations. In the North Zone, Colonel Gilbert Renault's (1904-1984) (known as "Raymond" or "Ro" or "Rémy") was tasked with the development of such secondary networks, just like Pierre Fourcaud (1898-1998), called "Barbes" did in the South Zone, where he contributed to the establishment of many networks especially between 1940 and 1941.

THE MISSION OF "RÉMY":
ONE ACTION, MANY LESSONS

It seemed that Colonel Rémy's mission has played a crucial role in the development of a whole network of informant in the West of France and of liaison with Spain. Through relationships, especially with the consul of France in Madrid, Jacques Pigeonneau, Rémy managed to convey to London intelligence on the German

(continued on page 79)

---

5. Most of the team returned to Britain from Saint-Gilles-Croix-de-Vie aboard a submarine, on the night of 4 to 5 April. Only Joel Tac remained in France.

Top.
A Lysander which came to grief on 31 August 1942 during operation Boreas II on the "Faisan" landing strip 1,8 km North of Arbigny near Pont-de-Vaux. Having received faulty landing guidances, the Lysander did a hard landing, breaking both its landing gear and propeller. The pilot, squadron leader W.G. Lockhart DSO, DFC and his passenger, Pierre Delaye (who was killed by the Gestapo on 11 May 1943) were not hurt in the accident. The Lysander was torched and Lockhart managed to return to London on 13 September 1942.
(Jean-Michel Rémy picture)

Right and center.
Accountancy book, (credit requests) of Section F.C. of the BCRAL dated January 1944.
(Archives Nationales document)

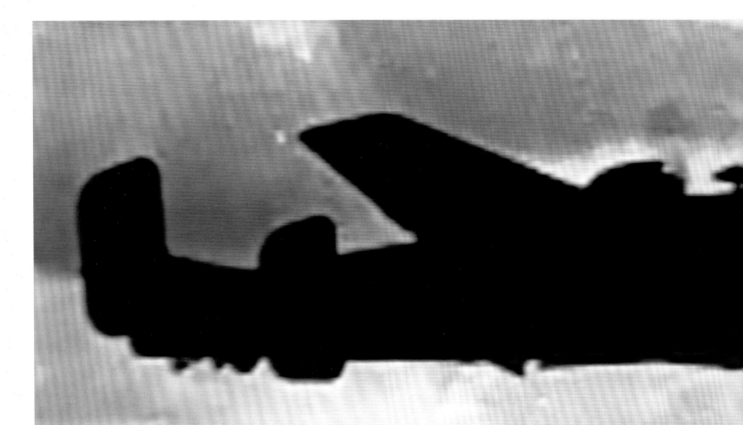

Parachute and pick-up operations
Decisive air support

During the month of August 1941, blind (that is without a reception committee) parachute operations were abandoned

The vitaly important parachute drops brought weapons, ammunition, explosives, identity papers, money, etc. to the networks and they generally took place on full moon nights in order to make it easier for the pilots to locate their dropping zones. The availability of aircrafts, which was already placed under great strain by the British services, was sometimes a problem. Until early 1943, the most commonly used aircraft was the Lysander but by 1942, only four Lysander were available to the Tangmere-based squadron, which was tasked with supporting résistance networks in occupied territories. Whitley bombers were also tasked with parachute operations. On any given full moon night, 60 to 80 sorties were flown in support of the different services including probably fifty over France. Of these fifty flights, only half were in support of BCRA operations. Given the importance of air operations, on the night of 10 to 11 June, 1941 Lieutenant Mitchell, a.k.a "Brick" who was in charge of the Evasion Section of the BCRA was sent to France in order to locate and list possible landing zones (LZs) and dropping zones (DZs). The choice of landing zones met strict selection criteria; they had to be approved by the Royal Air Force (RAF), even more so from 1942 on with the increase of air operations. Motorboats and fishing vessels were also used to recover agents or escapees. The RAF even established a map of France with all the reliable LZs and DZs.

The DZ, often in the form of a "L", had to be six hundred meters long with a width of three hundred meters. DZ marking was performed using flashlights or fires. The BBC (British Broadcasting Corporation) played a crucial role in transmitting messages, confirming to the local networks the day and the time of planned airdrops. Danger was never far; the gendarmerie, the French Milice, or even a detachment of German soldiers of the Wehrmacht or Waffen SS could always appear at the worst possible time and the plane could always be hit on its way in or out by the German Fliegerabwehrkanone (Flak).

The dropping phase itself obeyed a strict sequence: the first to jump was the radio operator then the mission commander on the second run, and finally the third member if there was one. The other option was to jump one after the other on the same run but this led to loss of time during the regrouping phase on the ground.

Add to that the uncertainties generated by agents being dropped either too high or too far from the intended DZ, on difficult or marshy terrain not to mention containers being scattered on landing and it becomes fairly obvious that the parachute insertion of agents was fraught with all kinds of dangers.

From 1941 on, pick-up operations became more common. They normally were conducted in support of the following kind of personnel: downed pilots, escaped prisoners of war, résistance fighters on the run or agents with blown covers. They all needed to be safely brought back to the United Kingdom.

Left and bottom.
A 138 Squadron Halifax in
flight over France.
(Now it can be told documents)

In general, the pick-up took place between 23 pm and 2 am, on a marked LZ, using a pre-defined code-letter as authentification methodPick-up operations also allowed the delivery of heavier loads; for example, on 27 February 1942, Rémy arrived in France with nearly 50 kilograms of documents, including forged identity cards and passes.

Note: For more details, refer to the works of Jean-Louis Perquin: *The Clandestine Radio Operators and Clandestine Parachute and Pick-up Operations,* editions Histoire et Collection.

Previous page top.
During a Hudson pick-up, the passengers walk towards the aircraft.

Previous page center.
A member of a maquis belonging to a reception committee holding an SOE torch during a landing strip marking operation.

Top.
November 1944, Lysander Mk III SD R 9125 piloted by Turner in flight. This plane is currently the only 161 Squadron survivor. It is on show at the Hendon RAF museum, unfortunately without its additional, long-range fuel tank. The ladder has been repainted in the Army camouflage pattern but the rear cockpit is still in the SD configuration.

Bottom.
A Hudson taking off during a full moon agent pick-up operation.
(Now it can be told documents)

A team of BCRA agents on the tarmac of Tempsford RAF base. The mission leader and his female liaison officer have donned their parachute equipment and are ready to emplane the 138 Squadron Halifax which is going to drop them over occupied France.
(Original work by Joachim Pol)

armed forces' military installations and their potential from Quiberon to Bordeaux. Although, his informants were not professional, they still managed to provide crucial intelligence reports. To ensure that the intelligence, which had been collected at great risk, would soon make its way to London, it quickly became necessary to provide the officers with radio transmitters[6]. The transmission of those intelligence reports was crucial but it often suffered from bad reception or transmission caused either by the mishandling of the radio sets which led to broken parts or simply by a weak signal or bad reception. However, Rémy's network could pride itself of the fact they were operating no less than six of the only twelve radio sets the Free French intelligence service (SR) then had in its inventory. As far as finances were concerned, the networks of Rémy, Saint-Jacques and Fourcaud (the Froment network) received nearly 20 million francs from the British.

On January 1941, at the request of General de Gaulle, it was decided to expand the network established in the West of France from Caen to Dunkirk and Paris. "Saint-Jacques" was responsible for this vast program. Parachuted in Dordogne, near Bugne, with his radio operator, "Saint-Jacques" injured himself on landing (broken leg). He was finally arrested and interrogated by the gendarmerie and by officers of the Bureau des Menées Antinationales (Antinational Actions Bureau

or BAM)[7]. He managed to talk his way into persuading them that he was from the Deuxième Bureau of the Vichy regime and that he was just returning from Great Britain. He managed to get to Paris and then to move into the unoccupied zone.

The first months of 1941 still showed some signs of amateurism in the way operations were being carried out but this was gradually corrected. The missions were therefore prepared with the utmost care. They had a clear purpose, the financial means were allocated, the personal qualities and skills of the agents selected for the tasks were assessed, and finally the infiltration and exfiltration routes were determined. A particular attention was also

Top.
"In" passengers boarding a
161 Squadron Hudson.
(Now it can be told document)

Top.
Dropping zone marking as
seen from the pilot's cockpit.
(Now it can be told document)

6. On this critical issue, refer to the work of Jean-Louis Perquin, *The Clandestine radio operators. SOE, BCRA, OSS*. Paris, éditions Histoire et Collections, 2011, 111 pages.
7. The BAM was created by a decree voted on 8 September 1940. Its mission was to protect the armed forces against the so-called " anti national activities ". The BAM had nine offices in France (Bourg-en-Bresse, Chateauroux, Clermont-Ferrand, Limoges, Lyon, Marseille, Montpellier, Toulouse and Paris) and three others in North Africa (Rabat, Algiers and Tunis). The head office of the BAM was located in Marseille. The BAM was disbanded in March 1942 and replaced on 24 August 1942, by the Service de Sécurité Militaire (Military Security Service or SSM) under the direction of Major Paul Paillole, who previously headed the BAM. With the occupation of the South Zone, the SSM officially stoped existing but a covert branch survived in Algiers.

paid to the different individuals who were supposed to be contacted when in occupied territory and to the quality of the communication systems. Everything was subject to the approval of General de Gaulle. His consent was translated into a signature of the mission order, and the operation was then launched.

In order to improve the communications between occupied France and the United Kingdom, Passy decided to send Captain Pierre Julitte MBE (1910-1991), a.k.a "Joly" or "Guy" to France. During the night of 10 May 1941, Julitte, who was a radio engineer by trade, jumped into France with his own radio set after a brief parachute training course. There, he was responsible for contacting the various networks and to report on the malfunctions in communications. He should thus help to establish better connections between the networks as well as with London. He also recruited radio operators on site and trained them and, for security reasons, proposed to establish independent communication networks. The British initially rejected this proposal before it finally was implemented in 1943.

In "Rémy's" network, after an initial shake up of the system, the communication achieved a good rate of success with over thirty messages sent to London in a month. In order to speed up the process, it was also then decided that the networks would use the English codes when the intelligence report was dealing with military or technical issues. When intelligence reports dealt with French administrative and political issues, they were sent using a French code. Rémy, thanks to a careful network of intelligence agents, managed to transmit a valuable estimate of the German battle order of the forces located on the coastline of France, from the Bay of the river Seine to the Spanish border. But he lost his radio operator, Bernard Anquetil – code name "Lhermite" – who was arrested in Saumur in July 1941 and shot by firing squad in October without having spoken under torture.

By the end of 1941, the French Secret Service operated a dozen covert radio stations and 29 agents were deployed in France. Five of them were killed or imprisoned during their mission. The BCRA could also rely on several strong networks, such as the Confrérie Notre-Dame (CND), which had nearly 2,000 members but which was soon to be destroyed. In 1943, 537 of the 1,135 members of the CND network were arrested. Among them, 257 were deported or shot[8]. Until 1943, the BCRA considered the CND as its main relay in France. It sent a considerable number of reports that were the source of many useful intelligence finds for the Allies. The British services were financing the CND to the value of up to 5 million francs per month.

The radio operators were particularly at risk as they were exposed to German direction finding units[9] as well as to the so-called "gonioconcierge", i.e the gossip and careless talks that could betray the efforts of covert operators. According to the SOE, loose talks were responsible for nearly 4/5th of the arrests[10]. Thus, in 1941 and 1942, nearly 75% of the radio operators were arrested; some were deported while others were killed[11]. In 1943, despite tangible progress in training and security procedures, 50% of them were still neutralized by the Germans[12].

Despite disagreements within the services, the French and the British worked together on several occasions. Thus, in May 1941, the Josephine B operation was launched in the Pessac and Bordeaux region. The mission aimed at the destruction of a power plant which were supplying heavy industries in the Bordeaux region as well as the submarine base. The operation reflected the collaboration between the BCRA, the SOE and the Royal Air Force. It was supervised by André Dewavrin ("Passy"), Major R. H. Barry from the SOE and the head of the RRF SOE section, Eric Piquet-Wicks. The British had suffered a failure during a previous operation in April, with a Polish sabotage team. This time, three

Frenchmen, Sergeant Forman, Second-Lieutenants Varnier (demolition expert), and Cabard were parachuted during the night of 11 to 12 May 1941. At first, they did not manage to destroy the plant and to reach the meeting point near Mimizan where they were to be retrieved by a submarine in time. As they remained hidden in the area, they were then joined by Joel Le Tac. Forman and Le Tac had already operated together during Operation Savanna. During the night of 7 to 8 June 1941, the four of them managed to destroy six of the eight station transformers, rendering it inoperative for several months. The team then reached the South Zone but the Lysander pick-up, which had been scheduled for the evening of 8 August, had to be cancelled. The agents then had to take the long route back to the United Kingdom through Spain.

FAILURES AND TREASONS: TWO CONSTANT COMPANIONS.

Some of the early operations suffered tragic failures. Often, the selection process of the incriminated agent had not been thorough enough or they did not meet the expectations when deployed on operation.

Navy Lieutenant Honoré d'Estienne d'Orves (1901-1941) a Polytechnique graduate who had joined the Deuxième Bureau in late September 1940, was sent to France on 21 December of the same year.

He was betrayed by his radio operator, an Alsatian by the name of George Marty who was a member of the German counter-intelligence services, with whom he was landed from a sailboat on 22 December 1940, near Plogoff in Brittany. Their mission, which was decided by General de Gaulle against the advice of Passy and Admiral Muselier, was to establish an intelligence network first in Nantes and then in the Paris region: the Nemrod network. D'Estienne d'Orves was arrested on 21 January 1941, as dozens of other members of the Nemrod, and was shot on 29 August 1941, at the Mont Valerien Fort near Paris with two other members of the network, FFL Second-Lieutenant Maurice Barlier and a Dutch national named Jan Doornik. To this day, Lieutenant de Vaisseau D'Estienne d'Orves remains the first Free French to have been executed by firing squad by the German armed forces. The irony is that his radio

set, code named Athos, was the only one which functioned properly during this mission but it was destined to remain in German hands.

Another operation also demonstrated the constant betrayal threat. At the end of April 1941, after Denys Boudard and Jean Hébert had managed to enter the Caen-Carpiquet air-base used by the Luftwaffe to seize a Bücker Jungmann aircraft, the British services requested the BCRA to carry out an intelligence gathering mission on the same airfield in order to prepare for a future British-led sabotage mission. This mission was to be the first intelligence gathering mission of the BCRA.

Called "Mission Torture", the operation was launched during the night of 8 to 9 July 1941, with two agents, both belonging to the Free French Air Force: Second Lieutenant Henri Labit, a.k.a "Mabil" or "Leroy" and

---

8. Guy Perrier, *Le colonel Passy et les services secrets de la France libre*. Paris, éditions Hachette Littératures, 1999, page 95.
9. In the occupied zone, the mission to locate covert radio was given to the German signal counter-intelligence service, the *Funkabwehr*.
10. Instruction No. 229 from the SOE towards the radios in France. "Précautions générales à l'usage des radions en France." Private Funds Pierre Lassalle. Quoted by Robert Belot, Gilbert Karpman, " La circulation du renseignement clandestin dans la résistance : enjeux politiques et techniques de la cryptographie" in Fabienne Mercier-Bernadet (dir.), *1939-1945 ; La guerre des intelligences*. Paris, éditions Lavauzelle, Collection " Renseignements et guerre secrète ", 2002, page 291.
11. For example, of the 28 radio operators trained in Inchmery House and parachuted in France between 1941 and 1942, 26 were captured by the Germans, of whom 16 were deported, 9 were killed and one was imprisoned.
12. Percentages given by Guy Perrier. Cf. Guy Perrier, *Le colonel Passy et les services secrets de la France libre*. Paris, éditions Hachette Littératures, 1999, page 118.

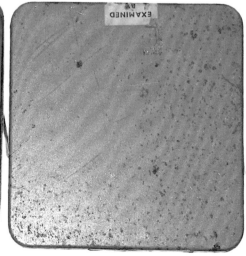

Left.
The Croix de la Libération. More than a decoration, this cross was to be the visible symbol of an Order created by General de Gaulle from the very beginning of the Résistance. The order became a reality on 29 January 1941 when the first five " compagnons de la Libération " were awarded. Those same five awardees became the first five members of the Ordre de la Libération council. Ninety percent of the Compagnons de la Libération joined the Fighting French before 1942. Three quarters of those were " résistants of 1940 " but joining the Free French early was not the only pre requesite; the awardee had to have performed acts of great bravery or to have performed distinguished service. Self-sacrifice was also taken into consideration as witnessed by the 271 posthumous awards of the Croix de la Libération. Those strict rules were not to be bent and only a select few would eventually receive this decoration, underlining its exemplary value. A total of 1,053 Croix de la Libération were awarded. Sixteen were collective awards to military units or vessels and five went to cities, towns or villages: Paris, the Sein island (Ile-de-Sein), Grenoble, Vassieux en Vercors and Nantes.

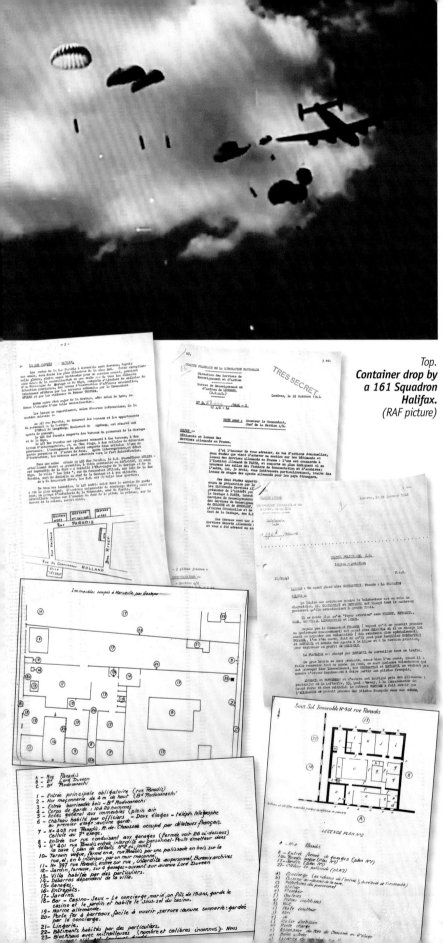

Corporal Jean-Louis Cartigny a.k.a "Geneste." The two men were parachuted near Carpiquet. According to a plan developed in June, their mission was to make contact with a local résistance network, the Groupe Frémont, led by a war veteran who had given his group his name, and who had expressed his willingness to take the fight to the enemy. The two BCRA agents' task was to assess the support the group needed to conduct offensive actions.

It was also expected of Labit to structure the network into several branches and to get them to conduct operations in support of the French and British services. Finally, they also were tasked with the selection of dropping zone for covert airdrops. They had no time to carry out those tasks as they were soon arrested by the Germans after having been betrayed by a local electrician. Their parachutes were found and Frémont questioned. Only Henri Labit escaped while Jean-Louis Cartigny was tortured and finally executed in April 1942. So was Frémont[13]. Labit continued to work with the BCRA in the Toulouse region until May 1942 when, in Langon, cornered by the Germans, he chose to swallow his cyanide pill.

These early missions were judged as relative successes if not failures, given the expected results.

However, the BCRA also had some genuine successes that had a real psychological impact. On the night of 9 to 10 May 1942, two BCRA agents, Paul Bodhaine and Henri Clastère, managed to destroy the large collaborationist Radio Paris transmitter in Allouis in the Cher Department. It had been installed in July 1939 but from July 1941, it had been used by the Vichy radio services to broadcast the "La Voix de la France" program towards the French colonies. The destruction of two of the four towers of the transmitter led to the disruption of the broadcast for about ten days and put a temporary end to the jamming of the BBC broadcast towards France which was also located in Allouis.

Top.
Container drop by a 161 Squadron Halifax.
(RAF picture)

13. Philippe Bauduin, *Sous-Lieutenant Jean-Louis Cartigny FAFL. Aviateur-parachutiste martyr. Caen-Carpiquet 1941-1942*. Éditions Apieton, 2004.

Left.
Different pieces of a target package produced by the BCRA related to buildings used by the Sipo/SD German Institute in Paris and Marseille. They were sent to London at the beginning of 1942. These sites were potential targets for the action teams of the BCRA. These specific documents were based on information gathered by an informer (alias La Fontaine) who had access to Pierre Costantini, one of the founders of the collaborationist Légion des volontaires français (LVF) movement.
(Archives Nationales documents)

In front of the townhall of the 7e arrondissement in Paris on 26 October 1944 on the occasion of Cécile Pichard and Jean Chassain de Marcilly's wedding.

In the foreground, Cécile Pichard a.k.a "Jacqueline Pradier" and "Altesse". She had been recruited as a P2 agent for the BCRA by her brother Michel Pichard MBE and taken to the United Kingdom by pick-up on 15 November 1943. After training as an agent, she volunteered for a mission in occupied France. She was parachuted in the area of Rivière-les-Fosses in the Côte d'Or département on 11 August 1944. Within the Anis mission, she performed multiple tasks, ranging from liaisons to the transportation of radio sets and weapons and the organization of parachute drops. She finished the war with the rank of Second Lieutenant and eleven month of active duty as a direct action agent. On the right, her husband, Lieutenant Jean Chassain de Marcilly a.k.a "Jean Lavernade", "Mecanique" and "Lieutenant Marc". Having previously served with the Corps Francs d'Afrique (a light infantry raiding unit), he then joined the BCRA in Algiers on 18 August 1943. Under the alias of "Jean Lavernade", he arrived in London on 6 October 1943. Volunteering for a mission in occupied France, he was tasked with the mentoring of the Pique en Pierre maquis in the Vosges département as part of the Chypre mission. He remained in command of the Gerardmer maquis until 15 October 1944 and finished the war with the rank of Captain. Behind the bride and groom can be seen, from left to right, Captain Puech Samson DSO operations officer of the Free French 2 SAS who fought in Africa, France and Holland; Marguerite Petitjean, a.k.a "Binette" a BCRA agent who was parachuted over occupied France and who received no less than five citations on her Croix de Guerre; Major Michel Pichard MBE, military delegate of Region P3, East, in command of air operations for this region ; unknown ; Lieutenant Christian Longetti MBE, Region C1 operations officer in occupied France. (Longetti family picture)

The United Defense M42 9X19 mm submachine gun
Designed before the war by Carl G. Swebilius, it was produced by the New Haven-based Marlin Company in 1942. Initially ordered by the Dutch government, the batch was finally purchased by the OSS. Some of the weapons were then provided to the SOE in order to be dropped in Europe in support of résistance movements. The finish of this weapon was better than what could be found on most other SMGs of the period but this quality came with a price and only 15,000 UD M-42 were finally produced.

The Sten MK II 9X19 mm submachine gun
No other weapon was dropped in larger quantities to résistance movements than the Sten. It was designed in April 1941 by Reginald Vernon Shepperd and Harold John Turpin, hence the name: S for Shepperd, T for Turpin and EN for Enfield: the Sten was born. Mass production started in June 1941; by 1943, 47,000 Sten were produced a week and at war's end, a total of 3,750,000 Sten SMG had been delivered.

The Bren Mk I Light Machine Gun
a.k.a the "Bren-Gun"
The Bren was a Czech LMG adapted to the British 0.303 round and licence-built at the Enfield arsenal. It was arguably one of the best designs of its time, its only drawbacks being that it was fed from an overhead magazine which meant that the sight line was offset to the left, making it virtually impossible for a left handed shooter to operate the weapon.

The Enfield N° 2 MK I revolver
This revolver was a simplified version meant for wartime production of the British Army issue revolver. It was parachuted in large quantities to the different résistance movements. Calibre: 380 MK II (9.65 mm).

The M1 "Bazooka".
In 1942, using a 60 mm mortar as a basis, American weapons engineers under the command of Colonel Leslie Skinner, designed the M1 Rocket Launcher. In May 1942, the US Army had received 5,000 M1s. The "Bazooka" nickname was given to this weapon because it bore a resemblance to the instrument an american artist by the name of Bob Burns had popularized around the same period. Calibre: 60 mm.

(Defense Museum Oslo pictures, Jean-Louis Perquin)

The M1 carbine.

The M1 carbine was a gas-operated weapon, which was initially intended for rear-echelon and support troops; its design was based on the M1 Garand but in a different calibre (.30 Carbine or 7.62 x 33 mm). Light and easy to handle, its main drawback was its lack of stopping power and its range which was limited to a maximum of 150 meters. Mass production started in September 1941 and issues started in July 1942. Airborne units received the folding stock M1A1 version. About 9,000 M1carbines were dropped by the SOE and some M1A1 also found their way into France. Just like the Colt 1911A1 pistol and the Thompson SMG, the M1 was seen as a "prestige" weapon by the Allied services.

The Welrod MK. II.A suppressed pistol

The archetypal secret service weapon, used for the execution of traitors and the close protection of radio operators. It was one of the very few completely silent weapons...
The Welrod existed in two calibres:
7.65 Browning (.32) et 9 mm Parabellum (.38)
An SOE document reported that after a 22 June 1943 meeting, an assassination campaign targeting Gestapo and SS officials in occupied Europe was decided. The Welrod was to be the main tool of that program and 600 were ordered, 100 having to be delivered as early as July...

The 82 grenade or Gammon bomb

This grenade had been designed as a high explosive, hand-thrown, impact detonation, instant fuze device. It consisted of a material bag, a metal cap, an 'Allways fuze' (the same fuze as found in the No. 69 grenade) and up to 900 grams of composition C explosive. Metal scraps were sometimes added in order to improve its efficiency against troops in the open. Parachuted in large quantities to résistance movements, it usually made a strong impression on German troops who often thought they were subjected to mortar barrages when on the receiving end of Gammon bombs.

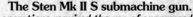

The Sten Mk II S submachine gun.

Some special operations required the use of suppressed weapons, leading to the design of special version of the Sten gun, the Sten Mk II S. This version had a maximum range of about fifty metres, since the muzzle velocity of the 9 mm round was limited to less than 300 meters per second. The Sten Mark II S was arguably one of the most succesful suppressed weapon ever to be produced, to such an extent that the Americans produced a copy of the Mk II S in the sixties in order to use them in Viêt-Nam!

The Projector, Infantry, Anti Tank (PIAT)

In order to replace the "Boys" Mk I antitank rifle which only was efficient against armour less than 10 mm thick, British weapons engineers designed a new antitank weapon which combined spigot mortar and rocket launcher technology as well as some aspects of the "Boys" Mk I. The end result was called the PIAT for Projector Infantry Anti-Tank.

This weapon remained less than perfect but was never improved during the war. Among its main design flaws were the fact that the trigger had to be pulled with four fingers and the extreme sensitivity of the round, which could detonate prematurely if not handled carefully. Calibre: 89 mm.

Free French (FFL) para wings

For obvious operational security reasons, a specific BCRA badge was never designed. Officiers usually only wore a french armed forces uniform with a Free French insignia. The only specific badge were the parachute wings. Captain Passy had demanded that, to be part of the *2ᵉ Bureau*, officers had to be parachute qualified since they could be sent on operational missions in occupied France with a very short notice. Initially, British para wings were worn but then the Free French wings were awarded to the airborne qualified officers who joined the BCRA. This insignia originated from the *1ʳᵉ compagnie de chasseurs parachutistes* and it was initially designed by Captain Bergé OBE MC and less than a hundred copies were produced in November 1941 in the Levant. The woven version appeared in the Spring of 1942 and became the Free French para wings, the only Free French insignia which could be worn above the left pocket of the uniform, on top of the ribbons.

THE BCRA MISSIONS
Creating a combined intelligence and action network

By DEFINITION, a resistance network represented an organization the main task of which was to provide intelligence while working underground, with no real external link, with the outside world except some radio communications, airdrops and from time to time the reinforcement of an additional agent. The decision to create the network was taken outside France either by the FFL or by the British special services. It coul also be tasked with secondary missions such as for sabotage and pick-up operations. If the networks were largely depending on the UK for weapons and funds deliveries, they nevertheless

Top.
A 138 Squadron Halifax dropping containers.
(Now it can be told document)

Left.
On 14 July 44, Maurice Mercier "Péruvien" who had been recruited in France in early 1942, operates an S-Phone 13 Mk III during Operation "Cadillac" on DZ "Taille-Crayon" (pencil sharpener) located in Vassieux en Vercors. On that day, 72 B17 dropped 862 containers.
(Au cœur de l'orage picture)

remained strictly independent from each other, in order to ensure the survival of the different networks.

On the contrary, the résistance movements were naturally and spontaneously created, thanks to highly motivated individuals, driven by the same patriotic convictions and driven by the willingness to take the fight to the enemy and by a strong resistance spirit. The concept of the compulsory labor service (Service du travail obligatoire - STO) encouraged a large number of young French people to join the Résistance or the maquis. Young résistance fighters sometimes followed friends or relatives who, just like them, were motivated by the fight against the occupation forces and the collaborators and who could no longer stand idle in front of shortages, restrictions, persecutions ... Unfortunately, their drive was not always compensating for their amateurism. Nevertheless, a great number of résistance fighters demonstrated ressourcefulness, physical and mental courage.

General de Gaulle's secret services needed to have a clear picture of the different movements and networks in France in order to assess them. Those networks provided two main types of intelligence products: political intelligence and military intelligence. Political intelligence focused on the Vichy government and on the activities of the Milice and of the collaborationist circles. As for military intelligence, it aimed at providing accurate and consistent intelligence on the positions and movements of the opposing forces, sometimes with reports requiring immediate action (troops and equipment transport, troop concentrations, operational

Top and right.
Maquis members recovering containers after a drop.
(Now it can be told document)

Bottom.
The Lysander of John Nesbitt-Dufort DSO after its crash in Issoudun on 28 January 1942 during operation Beryl. On this occasion it was transporting three agents, Roger Mitchell, Julius Kleeberg and Maurice Duclos OBE, MC a.k.a "Saint-Jacques".
(Collection Jean-Michel Rémy picture)

Joseph Monjaret
a.k.a "Hervé"

On 18 June 1940, Joseph Monjaret decided to reach England on board the trawler Queen Astrid from the port of Loguivy-de-la-Mer. He enlisted in the FFL on 1 July 1940. He first served with Major Berger's paratroopers. Then, just like Raymond Fassin, he joined the personal staff of General de Gaulle and the BCRA in June 1941. He soon met "Max" (Jean Moulin) even though he initially did not know of his real name. His mission was to prepare covert operations in the occupied zone. During the spring of 1942, two other BCRA officers, Raymond Fassin and Paul Schmidt, working respectively with the Combat network and with Libération, assisted him. In September, at the request of Jean Moulin, Monjaret was tasked with the mission of liaison officer to the Franc-tireur movement. Monjaret was then assigned the code name "Hervé" in France and "Frit" for his contacts with the services in London. In France, he operated under the identity of a young medical student from the city of Lorient named André Jacques Le Goff.

His mission was then to strengthen the links between the Franc-tireur movement and the BCRA and to prepare direct action missions as soon as he had received the required para drops to supply his operational teams. On April 4, 1943, he was arrested in Lyon.

The Gestapo was extremely keen to catch him because some of his action groups had succeeded in destroying several direction finding vehicles, killing one member of the SS in the process. He was imprisoned and tortured for several weeks before being deported to Germany on September 21, 1943.

He was then transferred from camp to camp, from Saarbruecken to Mauthausen before reaching a labor camp in the Vienna region. He survived this tragic journey and returned to France on May 4, 1945.

(Musée de l'Ordre de la Libération picture)

The Vélite-Thermopyles network

This network focused on intelligence gathering and answered directly to the BCRA. It was created in October 1940 by three professors of the prestigious Ecole Normale in Paris: Raymond Croland, Albert Mercier and Pierre Piganiol.

In 1941, the intelligence network (which was initially called Couleuvre) took the name of Velite. In 1944 the network changed its name again to Thermopyles.

Initially, its main area of interest was the North Zone and only occasionally, after November 1942, the South Zone. It performed different types of operations: intelligence gathering on individuals guilty of denunciations to the Gestapo, pick-up and exfiltration of downed pilots, general intelligence gathering from various sources on rail and river traffic, German troops movements, counterintelligence, etc.).

The network never ceased to grow in importance and fielded nearly a thousand of members. But in 1944, it suffered heavy losses and was decimated. In February 1944, Raymond Croland himself was arrested and deported

The network had links with members of the intelligence service of the Swiss army. A large amount of documents transited between France and Switzerland before arriving to London.

activities on airfields, target packages for future bombings requests for resupply drops). A constant stream of intelligence reports was also sent to London on background intelligence such as industrial activities in support of the occupying forces (including weapon and gunpowder production), enemy order of battle and moral, fuel and supplies depots etc.

The action of the various networks had to be synchronized. This task was to be given to the BCRA with the support of Jean Moulin and several other secret agents.

CONTACT WITH THE RÉSISTANCE IN OCCUPIED FRANCE: JEAN MOULIN AND THE BCRA

From September 1941 to October 1942, essential links were established with the Résistance in occupied France; then, the Comité de Coordination des Mouvements ZNO (Coordinating Committee of the Movements in the non occupied zone) was set up.

The role of Jean Moulin, whose code name was "Rex" or "Max", was essential for the establishment of contacts between the BCRA and the résistance networks such as Combat, Franc-Tireur and Libération[1], including within the Free Zone (as it was called until November 1942). At the end of 1941, Jean Moulin also reached London in order to give General de Gaulle a situation update on the status of the different résistance movements. Then he was parachuted blind over Provence from a twin-engined Armstrong-Whitley of the Royal Air Force in the Fontvieille / Mouriès area, near Saint-Endréol, during the night of 1 to 2 January 1942. Two other officers jumped with him: Raymond Fassin a.k.a "Sif," and Joseph Monjaret a.k.a "Hervé" or "Frit". He was the radio operator, the operating officer as well as the private secretary of Jean Moulin. Prior to this mission, Fassin and Monjaret had received sabotage training; they also knew how to organize landing and parachute operations. For several months, Moulin and his companions worked tirelessly to unify the numerous résistance movements and networks of the Free Zone. During the following months, Monjaret received reinforcements thanks to the drop of five other BCRA radio operators: Gérard Brault, a.k.a "Kim", on 15 April 1942, André Montaut a.k.a "Dude", on 28 May 1943, Maurice Cheveigné a.k.a "Salm", on 30 May 1942, Jean Holley a.k.a "Leo", on 15 June 1942 and Charles Briand a.k.a "Pal" in July 1942. Then, Daniel Cordier, a.k.a "Beep", who became the private secretary of Jean Moulin for nearly a year, joined them.

A permanent liaison had to be established with the key resistance movements. From January 1942, Raymond

---

1. This movement also benefited from a BCRA agent, Leon Morandat, in charge to establishing a permanent and direct link with London.

(Musée de l'Ordre de la Libération pictures)

Fassin performed the functions of liaison officer with Combat, as did Paul Schmidt, a.k.a "Kim" for Libération. From September 1942 on, Moulin appointed Monjaret as liaison officer to the Francs-Tireurs Partisans group led by Jean-Pierre Lévy.

With Jean Moulin, they created the *Service des Opérations Aériennes et Maritimes* (Air and sea operations Department or SOAM), made up of three structures, respectively located in Lyon, Clermont-Ferrand and Toulouse. Their mission was, every single month, to identify sites capable of receiving resupply and agent drops. Jean Moulin's deputies found it difficult to have their authority recognized by the various resistance movements leaders; they were young (with an average of 30) and they were part of the BCRA which had the ambition to extend

(continued on page 99)

Top left.
Michel Pichard MBE in August 1944. Parachuted during the night of the 11 to the 12 of August as a département Military Delegate, he organized many parachute drops, providing weapons to nearly 5,000 maquis members. On the bottom of his left sleeve, it is possible to make out the " light bulb " parachute qualification badge awarded to parachutists not posted to airborne units.
(Josiane Somers picture)

Michel Pichard
a.k.a "Bel", "Gaus" and "Pic"

Born in La Rochelle, Michel Pichard started his military service in the artillery before being found unfit for further duties and discharged in April 1939. On mobilisation, he managed to be finally accepted in the armed forces and was sent to the artillery school in Fontainebleau. Following the armistice on 22 June 1940, he left his unit to try and reach the UK. He boarded a French Navy ship, La Boudeuse, which took him to French North Africa where he was posted as a reserve officer to the *63e Régiment d'artillerie d'Afrique* (RAA) (Meknès). Listed as a deserter in his former unit, he was demoted and jailed in October 1940. In July1941, on his third attempt, he managed to escape and walked to Tangier in five days. After two weeks in hospital to recover from dehydration, he managed to leave for London with British help. He arrived in August 1941and after the customary security checks, joined the Free French forces. After a month of training in Camberley, he was promoted once again to the rank of Aspirant. He then was posted to the BCRA but during agent training he injured his hand during a sabotage course which meant he was unfit for operational duties for six months. Posted once again to the BCRA he completed his agent training syllabus. From August 1942, he was considered as fully operational. Posted to the Confrérie Notre-Dame (CND) network, he landed on the South coast of Brittany in January 1943.

In just a few months, he held several different positions: first, with the Organisation Civile et Militaire (OCM) between March and May 1943 and then with the Bureau des Opérations Aériennes (BOA), in charge of training the reception teams and DZ preparation. His successes in the field meant that he was promoted as the national head of the BOA in July 1943.

In March 1944, his Paris office was located by the enemy and his staff arrested. He then returned to France and, from the city of Vesoul, started organising new teams.

After another stay in London, he was parachuted in Brittany in July 1944 and operated with the Free French SAS of the *2e Régiment de Chasseurs Parachutistes* (2e RCP). He then did another parachute jump into occupied France, this time in the Haute-Marne département as the département military delegate (délégué militaire départemental) in order to coordinate parachute drops to the FFI.

From September 1944, Michel Pichard was posted to the *Direction Générale des Etudes et Recherches* (DGER) until January 1946. He then left the service in order to start a civilian career.

(Musée de l'Ordre de la Libération picture)

(Musée de l'Ordre de la Libération pictures)

1943
The "Arquebuse-Brumaire" mission

The purpose of this mission was once again to unify résistance movements in occupied France. It was conducted by André Dewavrin's (a.k.a Passy and, for this mission only, "Arquebuse") and Pierre Brossolette, a.k.a "Brumaire". "Arquebuse-Brumaire" had a strong impact; it came in the wake of several Major events of the year 1942 such as the Allied landing in North Africa (Operation Torch, 8 November 1942) or Jean Moulin's efforts to foster the cohesion of the various résistance movements of the Southern Zone (Operation *Rex*) and to impose a Delegation of the Fighting French.

In London, de Gaulle, had been convinced by Pierre Brossolette. He had agreed that the process of coordinating the résistance movements, which had started in the South Zone, had to be extended to the North Zone. Brossolette appeared as an expert on the state of the résistance movements in the North Zone.

Such were the objectives of the Arquebuse-Brumaire mission developed by Pierre Brossolette and André Dewavrin. Its mission also was to ensure that intelligence, civilian and military actions were differentiated; it also was aimed at gauging precisely the different

Top.
Colonel Albert Eon and Passy in a car somewhere in Brittany. Colonel Eon, commander of the Aloès mission was supposed to have been inserted by pick-up but poor weather led to the cancellation of the operation. Undaunted, he decided to be dropped instead carrying out his very first parachute jump during the night of 4 August 1944!

Left.
During mission Aloès, Lieutenant Jacques Mansion, Passy (seated) and Major Bernard Dupérier OBE, DFC (standing) in Brittany. The three of them were parachuted on 4 August 1944 on the "Bonaparte" DZ during operation "Frederick 18" near Kerien in the vicinity of the city of Saint Brieuc.

résistance groups as well as the socio-economic groups which, in all strata of French society, could contribute, at the appropriate time, to a national uprising.

For this mission, Pierre Brossolette and André Dewavrin, the two most important personalities in the BCRA, were appointed as representatives of General de Gaulle and of the French National Committee (the idea was then to delineate the jurisdictional boundaries of the two structures that were more or less in competition). Their complementarity and their ability to work together were obvious strategic assets that offset the considerable risks to which they were exposed while operating in occupied France.

JANUARY 1943: START OF THE MISSION

During the night of 26 to 27 January 1943, Pierre Brossolette landed in a Lysander, which left him in the Issoudun region. He managed to reach Paris on 12 February 1943.

Unlike Jean Moulin, who had been briefed by Brossolette himself on the content of his own mission, Brossolette wanted to create in the North Zone a structure identical to the one which already existed in the South Zone. De Gaulle chose Jean Moulin's idea with the creation of a single Council of the Résistance on 21 February 1943. Dewavrin met Brossolette in Paris on 27 February after being dropped the night before in the Rouen region with a British officer, Captain Forest Yeo-Thomas a.k.a "Shelley," who operated for the SOE (Seahorse mission).

Their task was to evaluate the paramilitary capabilities of the North Zone Résistance networks, and to know the political projects and positions they were taking compared to those advocated by General de Gaulle.

Although he was aware of the reorientation of the mission (the establishment of a "single command"), Brossolette preferred to continue with the mission he initially had been given, namely the creation of a *Comité de Coordination de la Zone Nord* (Coordinating Committee for the North Zone or CCZN) created from Résistance movements and similar to the existing CCZS.

Their efforts spread over almost two and a half months and led to the partition of the politico-military intelligence operations, and the creation of a Staff for the Secret Army of the North Zone. They also created two radio networks called Coligny and Prométhée.

After a brief stay in London, Jean Moulin returned to France and met Brossolette in Paris, on 30 March. This misguided initiative has been criticized in comparison to the line established by de Gaulle. However, Jean Moulin, rather than starting from a blank sheet of paper, preferred to adapt to the circumstances as he was now speeding up the operations. Nonetheless, he finally managed to establish the Conseil National de la Résistance (National Council of the résistance or CNR) in May 1943.

Regarding Brossolette and Dewavrin, they flew back to London on a Lysander, on the night of 15 to 16 April 1943, accompanied by Yeo-Thomas.

Silk scarf used for message coding.
(Jean-Thomas Duclos collection)

Bottom.
British Type 3 Mk II radio suitcase also known as the Type B Mk II or simply as the "B" type. Designed for the SOE by Major John I. Brown in 1942, it was the best known and the radio suitcase of choice for long distances because of its power, which gave it a range of about 800 km. The emitter delivered 15W of aerial power and this could prove dangerous when emitting from an urban area. Tuning the emitter could also be tricky and its 13 kg weight sometimes made it less than popular with its users.
(IWM picture)

Bottom.
Escape and evasion map of the north of France, Belgium and Holland printed on silk.
(Jean-Thomas Duclos collection)

Maurice Duclos
a.k.a "Saint Jacques"

Maurice Duclos was mobilised on 22 August 1939 as a reserve Lieutenant and took part in the May-June 1940 combat operations in Norway. Being one of the very first French officers to have joined the Free French Forces on 1 July 1940, he was posted to the 2e Bureau of General de Gaulle private staff under the command of Captain André Dewavrin and then to the Intelligence Services *(Service de Renseignements)* which were to become the BCRA. Maurice Duclos was also one of the very first officers to be sent on operation into occupied France. On 4 August 1940, a motor launch landed him on the beach of Saint-Aubin sur mer in the Calvados département. Over a period of more than five months, without any communication system of support, Maurice Duclos travelled around France establishing contacts throughout the country including with members of the first Free French intelligence gathering network, the "Saint-Jacques" network. He returned to london on Christmas eve 1940 through Algeria, Morocco and Portugal.

Volunteering for a second clandestine mission, Maurice Duclos was parachuted with some communication equipment and a radio operator in the Dordogne département near Le Bugue during the night of 13 to 14 February 1941. Breaking both legs on landing, losing contact with his radio operator, he was betrayed by the doctor who had treated him. Arrested by the police and taken to the hospital of Périgueux, he was given proper treatment but also interrogated. His case

being dismissed thanks to pre-war connections, Duclos was freed after a month. He immediatly resumed his mission in spite of his injuries. On 1 March 1942, Maurice Duclos managed to returned to the UK thanks to a pick-up operation.

After the creation of the CND network, Maurice Duclos established some contacts with the OCM *(Organisation civile et militaire*, civilian and military organisation) resistance movement and became, from April 1942, the head of the *Section Action, Etudes et Coordination* (Action, Studies and Coordination Section) within the BCRA. Promoted to the rank of Captain in May 1942, he carried out several other missions in occupied France in order to organise strategic and tactical level sabotage operations. He was in particular tasked with the preparation of the Armada I, Armada II sabotage missions and with the destruction of dams on the river Saône. He also organised the plan Vert (Green plan) which aimed at destroying railroads, the plan Tortue (Turtle plan) in order to delay the movements of German forces and the plan Violet (Purple plan) to neutralise enemy telephone communications on D-day. Maurice Duclos carried out another five missions in North Africa and France where he landed for the last time in August 1944 in Port-en-Bessin with allied Special Forces. He then took an active part to the campaigns of Normandy, Belgium and Holland. Before entering Germany, Lieutenant-colonel Duclos created and commanded the A 220 Commando unit which was tasked with sabotage and intelligence gathering behind enemy lines.

Bottom.
RCD 31/1 "Sweetheart" receiver. Designed for clandestine use by Norwegian engineer Willy Simonsen in 1943, this very compact set, which could also receive BBC broadcasts was issued to reception committee commanders. It was powered by torch batteries that gave 50 hours of operation.
(IWM picture)

Bottom and next page bottom left.
Details of BCRA office accountancy books dated January 1944.
(Archives Nationales documents)

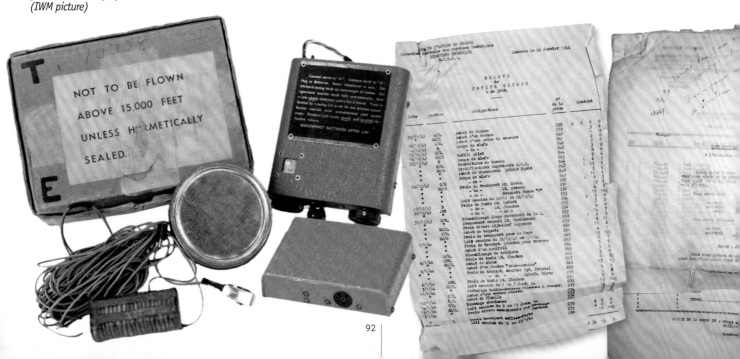

Charles Roger Hérissé
a.k.a "Lepic", "Dutertre" ou "Dunois"

Originating from the Eure département, Charles-Roger Hérissé participated in the Great War serving in a Moutain Infantry unit from April 1915. Wounded three times, he received three citations on his Croix de Guerre; he enlisted in the Air Force in February 1918 and obtained his pilot's license on a Nieuport aircraft on 18 August 1918. After the war, he continued to serve in the Air Force. He became a reserve officer in 1930, while continuing to be promoted: Warrant Officer II in 1923, Warrant Officer I in 1935, Second Lieutenant in 1936. He ended his career as a Major in December 1945. He then became a civilian pilot. He was a Lieutenant when war was declared in command of air base 129.

Demobilized when the armistice was signed, he joined the resistance in Amiens with the Alliance network (codename "Dutertre", number 89 044), which was part of the Confrérie Notre Dame (CND).

He was appointed mission chief. His responsibilities were expanded thereafter, especially since he fulfilled both the functions of Chief of Air Operations for the CND for regions M1 and P1 and Section Chief in the BCRA from 1941 to 1944.

He operated a network of nearly 25 agents and led a dozen air operations. He was in charge of the tactical and technical preparation of those air operations, including locating suitable Lysander landings sites.

He had a short stay in England in June 1943 and returned to France by sea in August of the same year, taking part in the Drome mission, in association with the Castille network.

When the CND was nearly anihilated following Tilden's betrayal, Hérissé managed to escape the Germans. From November 1943, he joined the Gallia network, led by Colonel Franklin. In July 1944, he returned to the United Kingdom. Soon after, he was assigned as a liaison officer to General Patton's 3rd U.S. Army Headquarters.

On 12 December 1944, he was posted at the Presidency of the Provisional Government of the Republic. On 29 October 1945, he was promoted to officier de la Légion d'Honneur. He died in Suresnes on 10 October 1974.

(Musée de l'Ordre de la Libération pictures)

Bottom right.
Bills handed over by a BCRA agent on his return to London after a mission in occupied France in October 1943.
(Archives Nationales documents)

Jean Moulin
a.k.a "Joseph Mercier", "Rex" then "Max"

Top.
A Whitley landing after a parachute drop mission. On 2 January 1942, Jean Moulin and his team were parachuted from that type of aircraft.
(RAF picture)

Left.
Jean Moulin a.k.a "Rex" in France in the Lyon region in 1942.

Jean Moulin, the son of a history teacher, was born in Beziers, France, on 20th June 1899. He was conscripted into the French Army in 1918 in the Engineer Corps but the First World War came to an end before he had the opportunity to see action.

After the war Moulin joined the civil service and rose rapidly to become the country's youngest prefect. He held a number of positions such as attaché to the cabinet of the Hérault département prefect, general counselor for the Hérault département, cabinet head for the Savoie département prefect (in 1922), sous-préfet of the city of Albertville (1925-1930) and then Châteaulin and sous-préfet of the city of Thonon-les Bains in 1933. Between 1934 and 1936, he was sous-préfet of the city of Montargis before being posted to the préfecture of the Somme in the city of Amiens as general secretary. Influenced by his friend, Pierre Cot, a radical pacifist, Moulin developed left-wing views.

Moulin refused to cooperate with the German Army when they occupied France in June 1940.

Just before the Second World War broke out, Jean Moulin had been appointed as the prefect of the Eure-et-Loir département. On 17 June 1940, he had his first brush with the German forces when he refused to incriminate members of the *tirailleurs sénégalais* (Senegalese Rifles, a french colonial unit) into the death of civilians in a place called La Haye, near Saint-Georges-sur-Eure. These civilians had in fact been killed by a German bombardment but Moulin was thrown in

Left.
During the night of the 1st to the 2nd of January 1942, Jean Moulin was parachuted in the Alpilles region near the city of Avignon along with his liaison officer Raymond Fassin and his radio operator Hervé Monjaret. On this picture, Moulin's holiday home in which he spent the night of 2 to 3 January with Fassin and Monjaret.
(Eric Micheletti picture)

jail nevertheless. He tried to slit his own throat so as not to be forced to incriminate the *tirailleurs sénégalais* but survived. He was sacked from his position on 2 November 1940 so decided to settle in the family house in Saint-Andiol, in the Bouches-du-Rhône département. From the end of 1940, Jean Moulin committed himself to the résistance and played a key role in the unification of the South zone résistance movements.

Moulin did several trip to London, arriving in the British capital for the first time in September 1941 from Portugal. General de Gaulle tasked him with the organisation of a secret army but insisted on the fact that the military and the political dimensions of the struggle had to be well delineated. Jean Moulin was integrated to the BCRAand met Passy and Jacques Bingen on several different occasions. His important political and administrative role did not spare him the rigours of agent training and he parachuted back into occupied France during the night of the 1 to the 2 January 1942 in the Alpilles region with funds and equipment. In his role as de Gaulle's general delegate, his mission was to bring a certain level of cohesion to the main South zone resistance movements (*Combat, Libération* and *Franc-Tireur*). He then set up his headquarters in Lyon. After a lot of difficulties, he managed to organise, in October 1942, the Armée Secrète (AS) which was placed under the command of General Delestraint, and then, at the beginning of 1943, the *Mouvements unis de Résistance* (Unified Résistance Movements or MUR).

After a short stay in London, he returned to France board a Lysander on 20 March 1943 under the alias of " Max ". From this date, he was the representative in France of the Comité national français (French national committee) and he managed to create the *Conseil National de la Résistance* (National Résistance Council). On 21 June 1943, while engaged in a meeting with several other résistance leaders which had been organised in Caluire-et-Cuire in order to find a replacement for the recently arrested General Delestraint, he was arrested by the German forces.

First tortured by the security police (SIPO-SD) in the Fort Montluc jail which was placed under the command of Klaus Barbie, and then in Neuilly by the Gestapo, he officialy died on 8 July 1943 in a train near Metz while being transferred to Germany in an extreme state of weakness.

Right.
The task General de Gaulle had given Jean Moulin on 5 November 1941 was to work towards the unification of the three main clandestine Résitance movements in France (Combat, Franc-Tireur and Libération) in order to persuade them to each create a military branch. In this plan, the centralization and the coordination was to be done in London under the orders of General de Gaulle.
(Jean Moulin museum pictures)

The *Confrérie Notre-Dame* network

In contrast to the generally accepted ideas about the political nature of the Résistance networks, the Confrérie Notre-Dame network owes its origin to men who were either monarchists or who placed themselves on the right of the political spectrum. They were staunch patriots and were hostile to compromises with Nazi Germany. The CND network was the first Résistance network to be created in support of Free France and it was one of the most effective.

Its founder, Louis de la Bardonnie, was a winemaker and lived in the Château La Roque in St-Antoine de Breuilh, in the Dordogne region. From June 1940, Louis de la Bardonnie, who chose "Isabelle" as his code name brought together a team of trusted relatives including Paul Armbruster a.k.a "Alaric", Pierre a.k.a "Pierrot", Simone Beausoleil, Dr. Gaston Pailloux a.k.a "Alceste," Paul Dungler and the abbot of Dartein, who was tutor of the heir to the French throne, the Count of Paris. It also was in the Château de La Roque that the very first FFL radio transmitter was set in February 1941. It is generally accepted that the first radio contact with London was established on 17 March 1941.

Louis de la Bardonnie decided to create a network dedicated to military intelligence and to send his intelligence reports to London. Initially, and even when the facts were cross checked, the allied services remained skeptical about the reliability of those reports dedicated to the German order of battle, to U-Boot identifications and which contained pictures of submarine bases.

At the end of November 1940, when the reliability of the CND network was proven, Gilbert Renault, a.k.a "Rémy", went to France and contacted the network, which by then numbered about thirty. "Rémy" already had decentralized intelligence gathering teams scattered over a large part of western France, equiped with staging points and "mailboxes" stretching across the demarcation line. Among these staging points were La Pallice (the La Rochelle harbour), Angoulême, Bordeaux, Bayonne, Pau, Toulouse and even Vichy.

Rémy decided that the Résistance movement created by de la Bardonnie would be called Confrérie-Notre-Dame in order to place it under the protection of the Virgin Mary.

The CND is considered as one of the first intelligence networks used by the BCRA. It became more powerful and gradually diversified the kind of intelligence it gathered, adding the economic and political dimensions to its intelligence requirements. The reports were then transmitted by radio from Thouars and Saumur, to London, or via liaison officers passing through Spain. The quality of the intelligence allowed the Allies to conduct strategic operations such as Operation Chariot, on 27 March 1942, which resulted in the destruction in the Saint-Nazaire harbour, of the only repair facilities on the Atlantic coasts capable of receiving the German battleship Tirpitz.

The effectivness of the CND eventually became a cause of concern for the Germans who spared no effort to neutralize it, mostly through the use of infiltration technique. Over the months the intelligence gathering operations became more and more dangerous and the number of arrests increased. Some, like Louis de la Bardonnie, were betrayed and, on 16 November 1941, arrested. Imprisoned in a Camp in Merignac, he was finally released in the Spring of 1942 because of a lack of tangible evidence against him. He remained a target for the Gestapo but always managed to escape the Germans, especially in 1943. Until the end of the war, Louis de la Bardonnie always seemed to be protected...

Other betrayals occured during the fall of 1943 and had a significant impact on the network because of the hundreds of arrests that they caused. Regardless, the CND always managed to rebuild its sub-networks, particularly under the leadership of Marcel Verrière a.k.a "Lecomte". The network was almost annihilated on several

Top.
Rémy onboard Les Deux Anges, one of the boats used to ferry Résistance members between the coasts of Brittany and waiting British motorboats that would then take them to the United Kingdom.
(Favier archives)

occasions but it still found the resources and motivation to recover and remain operational until the end of the Occupation.

Among its notable members was Charles Hérissé (1896-1974), a.k.a "Lepic", "Dutertre" or "Dunois" who was successively the mission head of the CND network and of a subgroup called Alliance with Charles Chauveau and Roger Dumont and who then became Chief of Air Operations of the CND. In 1942, the three of them were in charge of the target reconnaissance missions before Operation Biting, the destruction of the Bruneval radar station during the night of 27 to 28 February 1942. Between late 1941 and 1944, Hérissé operated as section head in the BCRA, commanding up to 25 officers. As such he was in command of a dozen air operations.

At the end of 1943, because of the pressure the German services put on him, Hérissé left the CND and switched to the Gallia network.

Depending on the sources and periods, the CND, called Castille from December 1943, fielded between 1,300 and 2,000 members. More than 1,500 people, (nearly 20% of them women) were recognized as full members after the war. German operations led to the arrest of 537 members of the network, among which 234 were deported (151 never to return), while 37 were shot. If, in the end, the network lost many of its agents, its founder survived the dark years and died in 1987.

Right.
The logbook of a Confrérie Notre-Dame radio operator.
(Document Archive Nationale)

Bottom.
Different make up styles tried by Rémy in London in October 1942 and in August 1943.
(Jean-Thomas Duclos collection picture)

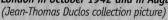

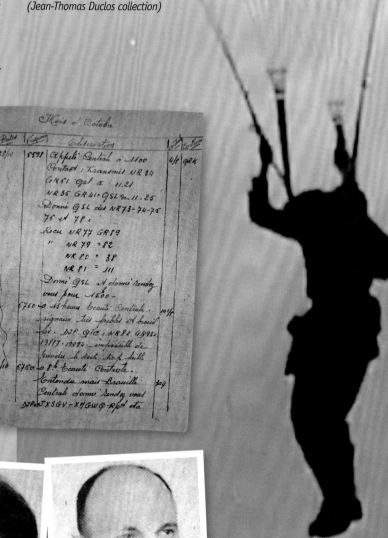

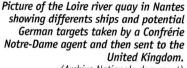

Picture of the Loire river quay in Nantes showing differents ships and potential German targets taken by a Confrérie Notre-Dame agent and then sent to the United Kingdom.
(Archive Nationale document)

Jean Ayral
a.k.a "Robert Gautier", "Guérin", "Robert Harrow", "Pal", "Major Roach", "Gedeon" and "Ceden"

Jean Ayral was born on 30 December 1921. After spending roughly two years in the Royal Navy as a Sub-Lieutenant, he accidentaly broke his leg and was given a shore position. After transferring to the Free French forces in October 1941, he then joined the BCRA in February 1942. After agent training in Inchmerry, he volunteered for a mission in occupied France. Parachuted on 26 July1942 in the Montluçon region under the nickname of "Pal" with François Briant his radio operator (alias "Pal-W") and Daniel Cordier (alias "Bip-W"), he was injured on landing. Nevertheless, he performed several intelligence gathering taks in the Clermont-Ferrand region until November 1942. Sent to Paris by Jean Moulin in order to liaise with his North zone representative Henry Manhès alias "Frédéric", Jean Ayral developed the "Pal" direct action network and met with several important players of the *Ceux de la Libération* (CDLL) and *Ceux de la Résistance* (CDLR) networks. With the support of those movements, he drafted a list of potential dropping zones. In April 1943, Jean Moulin tasked him with the creation of the North zone *bureau des opérations aériennes* (Air Operations Bureau or BOA). His deputies were Pierre Deshayes, Paul Schmidt and Michel Pichard, each one being responsible for one of the four regions of the North zone, Jean Ayral being in charge of the central region. Arrested in Paris by the Gestapo on 28 April 1943, he managed to escape with four other résistants who had been captured at the same time.

With his cover blown and under Jean Moulin's direct orders, Ayral had to return to London immediatly. He crossed into the South zone from where he managed to reach the UK thanks to an air operation on 16 June 1943. Promoted to the rank of Navy Lieutenant in January 1943, he was posted to General de Gaulle's private staff in Algiers as a BCRA officer. In early 1944, at the corsican base of the *Direction Technique des Services Spéciaux* (Technical Directorate of Special Services or DTSS), he created a service dedicated to covert maritime operations in support of French secret services activities in occupied Italy and France.

Parachuted 50 km North of Toulon in Brue-Auriac on 12 August 1944 as the commander of a 7-man commando team supported by a few FFI fighters, he attacked a German training camp situated near the Toulon to Marseille road, neutralizing between 150 to 250 soldiers. Jean Ayral was then the first allied soldier to enter the city of Toulon. Sadly, on 21 August at 15:45 hours, he was killed by friendly fire when a patrol from the *Bataillon de Choc* shot him with an SMG burst. He died the next day.

(Musée de l'Ordre de la Libération picture)

Next page.
Different pictures of the British submarine HMS Tribune operating in the Mediterranean. Within the frame of operation Sea Urchin, during the night of 4 to 5 February 1943, HMS Tribune landed a joint BCRA/SOE team in the Gulf of Valinco in Corsica. The team was made up of three agents: Fred Scamaroni DSO, Jickell and a radio operator.
(Royal Navy picture)

Bottom.
Between June 1940 and a mission carried out in the vicinity of Brest and November 1944 with a landing near Les Sables d'Olonne, British MGBs (Motor Gun Boat) operated in support of the SIS, SOE and BCRA in order to provide them with a covert infiltration/extraction service between Great Britain and the French coasts.
(Royal Navy picture)

its control on all movements and only leave them with very little room for initiative. Finally, the various movement leaders were engaged in power and ego struggles. Everyone tried to impose his own concept regarding the résistance, the type of operations that need to be conducted, the value of paramilitary actions against political actions, etc. To Jean Moulin, it was important to distinguish political activities from military actions and to create a network of leader at the local, regional and central levels answering to a single hierarchy. The political actions were based on two structures therefore implemented by Moulin: The *Bureau d'Information et de Presse* (Bureau of Information and Press or BIP) and the *Comité général d'Études* (General Committee for Studies or CGE).

The end result sought by Jean Moulin was to have, within occupied France, a series of network of reliable radio operators and teams of reliable résistance members capable of organizing parachute and landing operations. Jean Moulin played a crucial role in this matter by establishing, within the same structure, different services that were sufficiently compartmentalized and separated to guarantee such a level of operational security that it could resist betrayals, arrests and infiltrations.

From 23 April 1942, Passy and Pierre Billotte, General de Gaulle's Chief-of-Staff and Secretary of the National Defence Committee in London, agreed with the SOE for special action groups to be established in order to conduct raids targeting objectives that had been selected by the SOE. A few months later, on 14 October 1942, in order to accelerate the federation of the different Résistance movements and to assess the action and the needs of the intelligence networks in the unoccupied zone, the BCRA launched Operation Pallas. This name had been selected by Lieutenant Andre Manuel, the deputy of "Passy" in charge of the Intelligence Section of the BCRA.

Lieutenant Manuel, a.k.a "Pallas", was responsible for both a difficult and a capital mission. He also had been responsible for bringing the former ambassador of France in Ankara[2] René Massigli (1888 - 1988), to London[3]. In July 1942, Pierre Brossolette delivered Massigli a letter from General de Gaulle inviting him to join him in London in order to assume the position of Foreign Affairs Commissioner of the French National Committee. After some hesitation, he agreed, but due to a series of misfortunes and hazards, Manuel

(continued on page 103)

---

2. Under German pressure and following tensions between him and German ambassador Franz von Papen, the Vichy administration recalled René Massigli from his position in Ankara.
3. In 1919, Massigli was part of the peace conference staff and he also took part in several international conferences between the two wars. Without any official mandates between August 1940 and 1943, he was both close to the Vichy régime and against collaboration with Germany.

Top.
Re-enacted combat scenes prepared for propaganda purpose after the liberation of Corsica in October 1943. During the active phase of the campaign, the BCRA-A provided much needed help to the corsican résistance fighters.
(ECPAD picture)

Fred Scamaroni *a.k.a "Godefroy"*

Born in Corsica on 24 October 1914, Godefroy Scamaroni was the son of a senior civil servant. His family traditions were heavily influenced by patriotism, devotion to the country and sacrifice.

Fred Scamaroni read law in Paris, graduating in 1934. He did his military service as an infantry reserve officer.

In 1936, he became head of cabinet of a senior civil servant (Préfet) until the mobilization of 1939. Refusing opportunities to escape his duty, he served with the 119th RI (Infantry Regiment) on the northern front during the Phoney War.

Bored with the inactivity, which characterized the first part of the campaign, he requested a transfer and soon followed the training of air observer on the Tours air base where he got to know men who would become important figures of Free France such as Pierre Messmer, Roquère, Sainteny and Simon. During the Battle of France, he was wounded on 23 May, 1940 during an aerial combat, and received the Croix de Guerre. He also got promoted to Lieutenant.

After having recovered from his wounds he rejoined his unit. Refusing defeat and armistice, he decided to reach England. Once in London, he joined the FFL and was assigned to the St. Atham airbase, where he obtained his pilot wings. He then joined the personal staff of General de Gaulle.

During the raid which the Free French and the British carried out on the Vichy French base of Dakar, in Senegal, in September 1940, Scamaroni flew aboard a Firefly from the aircraft carrier Ark Royal, and landed on the Ouakam air base. He brought Governor General Pierre Boisson a letter from General de Gaulle but without any result. He was imprisoned with a few of his comrades and tried to escape during a transfer to Bamako but in vain. He was back in France and imprisoned in Clermont-Ferrand on 24 December, 1940, before being released in February 1941 after having been striken off the list of civil servants. Appearing to all as having seen the errors of his ways, he took up a position within the Supplies ministry. He soon started operating with different résistance networks such as Liberté and Copernic, even managing to get in touch with London through the American Embassy in Vichy.

On behalf of the BCRA and in connection with the SR of Marseille and London, he ran an intelligence gathering network from Corsica where he spent some time in the spring of 1941 and in October 1941 as well as some covert operations on mainland France. The Germans started getting interested in him after the Copernicus network was infiltrated and neutralized which meant he had to return to London on Christmas 1941. He then changed his identity and was from then on known as Captain "François-Edmond Severi."

JOINING THE BCRA

In early 1942, Dewavrin enlisted him into the Service Action of the BCRA. Scamaroni continued to run his corsican network, which provided intelligence on Vichy and Italian forces on the island and collecting data on possible dropping zones and beaching sites that were then transmitted to the RAF and the Royal Navy.

In November 1942 he went to Algiers via Gibraltar in order to provide intelligence reports on the situation on mainland France. Then, in January 1943, he returned with a two-man team (a radio operator, Jean-Baptiste

Top.
Joining form for the Free French forces in the name of François Séveri belonging to Fred Scamaroni DSO and, (right), a written order sending Captain Séveri into occupied France signed by General de Gaulle.
(Archives nationales documents)

Hellier a.k.a "Ambrose" and a British intelligence officer named Maynard a.k.a "Albert") to conduct sabotage missions and prepare weapons deliveries in Corsica, where they arrived in a British submarine on the night of 6 to 7 January 1943. Scamaroni's mission was also to unify the various resistance networks of the area. This proved impossible because of the reluctance of the different Communist résistance groups, such as Combat, FTP and Front National to establish regular contacts with London in order to plan their logistics support.

Scamaroni knew that a price had been put on his head. He used several aliases to make it more difficult for his opponents to locate him. Among his noms-de-guerre were "B13", "Chimère", "Edmond", "François Grimaldi", "Severi", "Pot" or "Sarment".

During his operations in Corsica, Scamaroni developed a strong network of agents and action groups supported by weapons, fuel and ammunition caches. Submarines conducted some of the resupply missions.

The R2 Corsica network was under stong pressure from the OVRA, the Italian fascist police. Many resistance fighters were arrested, tortured and deported. Hellier himself was betrayed and arrested on March 17, 1943. According to historian Louis Luciani, Salvatore Serra, an italian spy who was coming from Algiers and who had been arrested in Sardinia in the company of a British agent named John Armstrong, identified Hellier. The two men were transferred to Rome. Serra, eager to save his life at all cost, reportedly proposed to betray the Ajaccio résistance network and offered to identify Hellier. He said that Hellier could be recognized because he had eczema on the earlobe. Serra knew Hellier under the pseudonym "Louis" and had even trained with him.

Hellier was arrested in a cafe near Ajaccio and subjected to 30 hours of intense torture. It is commonly believed that he spoke and that his confessions led to the arrest of Scamaroni. Louis Luciani does not believe this version as Hellier was executed a few days later, while, according to him, the Italians did not shoot those who were willing to collaborate. In fact, according to the testimony of Virginio Sias, head of the Italian espionage in Corsica, the names of Scamaroni's landlords were found inside a tube of cream.

The Italians managed to arrest Scamaroni, alias Captain "Edmond Severi," on the night of March 18 to 19. He was imprisoned and tortured just like another eighteen members of the R2 network in Corsica. Rather than risking disclosing some vital intelligence under torture, Scamaroni preferred to commit suicide on March 19, 1943, in his cell in the Ajaccio citadel. He tore off his throat using a steel wire, his agony lasting hours. Without knowing his true identity, the Italians buried him in a mass grave. It was only in January 1944, once Corsica had been liberated that his body was exhumed and transferred to the Ajaccio cemetery.

"Fred" Scamaroni was honoured in several ways after his death. He was made a compagnion de la Libération by an 11 October 1943 order. He also was posthumously promoted to the rank of Préfet (senior civil servant with regional powers) by a decree dated 26 February 1945. He was posthumously awarded the Légion d'Honneur and the Croix de Guerre 1939-1945 while King George VI awarded him the Distinguished Service Order.

Left, top and next page.
Several pictures of the Free French submarine Casabianca. Between 1942 and 1943, she carried out 7 covert missions along the coasts of Corsica in order to insert of recover agents or to deliver weapons and ammunition to corsican résistance movements. On 13 September 1943, at 01:27 AM, the last of these missions saw the Casabianca landing 109 men of the Bataillon de choc (a Free French raiding unit) and a SOE/2ᵉ Bureau team in Ajaccio during operation " Vésuve ".
(Archives de la Marine nationale picture)

and Massigli did not return to England before 27 January 1943. Massigli served as Commissioner for French Equatorial Africa first at the French National Committee and then in Algiers in the French Committee of National Liberation (CFLN) (February 1943 - September 1944). This did not prevent many clashes between de Gaulle and Massigli, who had a certain freedom of speech and obstinacy, far from the image of the docile servant of the State he may have projected[4].

Manuel therefore gave his report with a significant delay since the conclusions were given back to de Gaulle on 8 February 1943. They nevertheless allowed to gauge some aspects of the French résistance. According to his findings, only 5% of the French were said to be active in the résistance and 40% could be considered as supporters of the FFL, against 55% classified as "idle" people. The latter comprized fence sitters, opportunists and those who were simply too paralyzed by fear to do anything.

The consolidation and synchronization of the actions of the different movements became more and more crucial as the Gestapo and Opera Vigilanza Repressione Antifascismo – (OVRA, the Italian counter intelligence services) put up more pressure on the résistance movements from November 1942, when the South Zone was finally occupied. For Manuel, as for Jean Moulin, it seemed obvious that the centralization of the networks had to apply to both the North and the

South Zones, even if the results were far from being guaranteed.

After the Pallas mission came the Arquebuse-Brumaire mission (see boxed text), which was conducted in 1943 by Pierre Brossolette, a.k.a "Brumaire" and André Dewavrin, who chose the "Arquebuse" nom-de-guerre instead of the usual "Passy". During some time, Churchill was opposed to Dewavrin taking part in any operation because that would have put the Free French services in a very difficult situation if he got captured or killed. Finally, de Gaulle managed to send Passy on an operational mission... The Arquebuse-Brumaire mission was run in parallele to the Pallas mission in the Northern Zone. It was covering the main resist-

[4]. René Massigli helped conforting Charles de Gaulle's credibility and the CFLN's diplomatic aura with both Churchill and Roosevelt. He was to become French ambassador to London between September 1944 and January 1955.

Top.
***A radio operator in the corsican bush (maquis in French). This picture and a film were taken a few weeks after the liberation of Corsica in support of the propaganda effort of the** Comité Français de Libération Nationale (CFLN).*
(SHD picture)

5. The OCM included resistants from the bourgeoisie, but also from intellectuals and academics circles as well as many professionals.
6. The FTP did not accept the situation as such because they wished to keep some flexibility in their actions before the Allied landings.
7. Guy Perrier, *Le colonel Passy et les services secrets de la France libre.* Paris, éditions Hachette Littératures, 1999, page 148.

ance movements of this geographical area: the Civil and Military Organisation (*Organisation Civile et Militaire - OCM*), created in December 1940[5], Ceux de la Résistance (CDLR), the Front National and the FTP, Libération-Nord and Ceux de la Libération (CDLL).

Upon their return, Brossolette and Dewavrin submitted their report. It was confirming that the creation of the Secret Army had been requested and that the résistance movements were now engaged in a unification process[6]. This led to the creation, on 26 March 1943, of the *Comité de Coordination des réseaux de résistance de la Zone Nord* (Coordinating Committee of the North Zone résistance networks), in addition to a *Conseil National de la Résistance*. Thus it was agreed that the various movements should therefore fall under the command of the staff of the Secret Army, established in October 1942, in the free zone and provide it with the required fighters. Each network, while keeping its autonomy in terms of political influence, had to be ready to integrate its paramilitary elements into the Secret Army for the sake of greater operational centralization and synergy. General Delestraint, who had everything

to learn in the field of covert operations, led the AS. His strength reached nearly 50,000 men in the North Zone against nearly 75,000 in the South Zone.

The National Council of Resistance (CNR), gathered for the first time on 27 May 1943. That same day, André Dewavrin was awarded of the Croix de la Libération, at the Ribbesford Ecole des Cadets, at the same time as René Pleven, Maurice Duclos, Pierre Fourcaud and Antoine Bissagnet.

1943: THE OPERATIONAL TEMPO INCREASES

1943 and 1944 saw a rgular increase in the number of operations. Their pace quickened and direct actions became more frequent.

To best meet operational requirements, on 24 April 1943, Passy organized a *Bureau des Opérations Aériennes* (Air Operations Bureau or BOA). Its task was to provide the BCRA with dropping zones throughout the French territory. In the spring of 1943, the BOA had proposed close to 500 dropping zones[7].

The networks and subnetworks remained vulnerable to infiltrations and arrests. From London, the French services were constantly replacing agents.

LA CORSE LIBEREE

l'ennemi a coulé en Corse : les collaborationnistes les plus dangereux ont été écroués. Les fonctionnaires dont le zèle s'est ... plus, c'est dans un sens populaire que l'administration est faite. La censure, par exemple, est exercée par une commission ... les patriotes font entendre ...

... les plus difficiles ... résolus à la ... C'est ainsi ... connaître la ... notamment du ... taillement des ... abandonnées ... grâce aux efforts ... néral Mollard, ... militaire de ... préfet Luizet, ... alliés, la situation ... male.

... foyers corses, ... par l'absence ... d'un étudiant, ... Après la débâcle ... la Corse ceux ... de toutes parts ... combattante, pour ... que ou la marine, ... née des 15.000 ... qui délivrèrent ... les troupes fran- ... formations spécia- ... rendra bientôt un ...

... re que bien ... France. La ... aîtres, ni les ... ires pro-fas- ... les Français ... la grandeur ...

A Ajaccio, le général de Gaulle déclarait le 8 octobre : "La victoire, nous l'aurons. Ce sera la victoire de la liberté."

Les patriotes corses écoutent l'allocution du Général.

A partir de ce ... officiers français ... œuvre pour assu- ... ment en armes de ... corse et pour me ... son organisation m ... moyens ingénieux ... troduire dans l'île ... bien qu'au début ... Résistance disposai ... stant de matériel ... de 3.000 hommes a ...

C'est alors qu ... faillit tout gâter ... d'un des comités ... coup de revolver p ... pendant qu'il din ... café d'Ajaccio. C ... prévu que le feu ... tôt, spontanément, ... qui risquait de se ... mettre. Des batai ... éclatèrent toutes ... un grand nombre ... chaque côté. Des ... mirent de la partie ... aux Italiens des v ... réunissaient les pa ... chefs du mouvem ... prendre le maquis ... dans les montagnes ... cachés dans les bo ... d'une vie frugale e ... La nourriture leur ... nuit par messagers ... que le contact était ... de nuit également ... quartier-général du ... en dépit de son âge, ... Giacobbi, qui avait ... avec d'autres patri ... dans un camp de co ... parvint à s'évader, ... heures avant le mo ...

Mitraillettes Sten, l'arme des forces de la résistance à l'oppresseur.

La Corse libérée sert de base offensive aux escadrilles de l'Aviation française.

L'emblème des patriotes corses flotte à côté des couleurs françaises.

Patriotes corses après la libération de leur territoire.

Attaquée par trois Allemands, cette jeune estafette de seize ans s'en est mit en fuite avec sa mitraillette et accomplit sa mission.

Elles ont combattu pour libérer la Corse.

EN CORSE LIBRE

Depuis deux mois, "l'Ile de Beauté" est délivrée. Elle n'est plus souillée par l'ennemi ni l'ex-ennemi. Comment donc ce fragment insulaire de la France s'est-il installé dans la vie nouvelle, la vie libre, la vie démocratique, la vie française ? Comment s'est fait le retour de la Corse à une existence digne de sa fidélité ?

Inutile de décrire l'accueil du peuple corse aux soldats français, au délégué du Comité de Libération Nationale, puis au général Giraud et au général de Gaulle. Partout ce fut un accueil fait de joie sobre et fière. Tous les témoins furent frappés par la ferveur des habitants, leurs yeux brillants, et la beauté de leurs rites de bienvenue, comme le jet de fleurs et même de riz (antique coutume) sous les pas de ceux qui représentaient l'unité française reconstituée librement, en terre libre. Mais ce qu'il est intéressant de connaître en toute précision, ne serait-ce que pour démentir les "mensonges qui font tant de mal à la France,"

et que répandent les délégués français de l'ennemi, c'est le calme, le bon sens, l'esprit de modération mais aussi l'enthousiasme avec lesquels la population, avant même l'arrivée du délégué du Comité de Libération Nationale, ont substitué aux créatures de Vichy des hommes, et même des femmes, élus à titre provisoire, dans chaque ville, chaque village.

Cette œuvre a été complétée depuis, et normalisée par le préfet Luizet, représentant le Comité de Libération Nationale. Partout, les maires et conseillers municipaux désignés par Vichy ont été remplacés par des patriotes de la Résistance. Bien plus, un Conseil départemental choisi parmi la Résistance, émanant de la population elle-même, siège à titre consultatif auprès du préfet. Quel contraste entre le régime autoritaire de Vichy et ce contact direct avec le peuple !

Ces solutions hardies n'ont été possibles que grâce à la modération des dirigeants de la Résistance. Seul, le sang de ...

A booklet and several pictures depicting the liberation of Corsica. They were parachuted over occupied France. Of note are the Sten SMGs arming most of the résistance fighters; they had been delivered by the Free French submarine Casabianca and Algiers-based 2e Bureau agents. *(Eric Micheletti collection)*

APPORTE PAR VOS AMIS DE LA R.A.F.

F. 165.

Cet opuscule a été jeté par centaines de mille sur la France métropolitaine par la R.A.F.

Despite multiple of arrests in 1943, the activities of the networks did not diminish, especially in the northern half of France (North Zone).

1943 saw an increase in sabotage and guerilla operations in the rear of enemy lines. The destruction of ammunition and fuel plants, power plants and power lines were also on the increase.

Communications were vitally important. To reduce the radio operator's vulnerability to German direction finding operations, a new security procedure was put in place, the Electra method. It consisted in the differentiation and compartmentalization of emissions and receptions; continual changes frequencies and codes; the use of highly trained radio operators. As the Allies also needed intelligence on the German troops movements and transit areas, the BCRA deployed up to 23 radio teams under the auspices of Plan PROFFA, which aimed at "regionalizing" intelligence gathering. Until 1944, the number of messages sent to London was increasing. In January 1943, 114 messages were sent monthly to France, on behalf of the Action Service in London. Their number increased to 910 in

Left.
Corsican résistance fighters after a series of combat operations against the last remaining German forces still present in the North of Corsica at the beginning of October 1943. From January 1943, London-based BCRA agents, then Algiers-based 2e Bureau agents operated in Corsica in order to equip and mentor the local résistance movements.
(Jean-Antoine Bichisano collection picture)

Bottom.
A Mills hand grenade on a multilingual SOE handbook on the use of weapons and explosives. This 171 pages (including 24 pages of sketches) booklet was written in six different languages and it was dropped with weapons' containers all over occupied Europe.
(François de Rochenoire collection picture)

BCRA agents arriving at RAF Harrington before departing on a mission to France.
(National Archives picture)

The structure of the secret services in September 1943

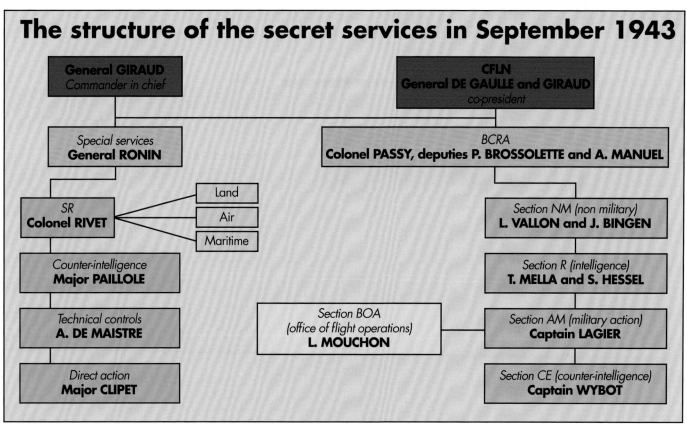

General GIRAUD
Commander in chief

CFLN
General DE GAULLE and GIRAUD
co-president

Special services
General RONIN

BCRA
Colonel PASSY, deputies P. BROSSOLETTE and A. MANUEL

SR
Colonel RIVET

Land
Air
Maritime

Section NM (non military)
L. VALLON and J. BINGEN

Counter-intelligence
Major PAILLOLE

Section R (intelligence)
T. MELLA and S. HESSEL

Technical controls
A. DE MAISTRE

Section BOA
(office of flight operations)
L. MOUCHON

Section AM (military action)
Captain LAGIER

Direct action
Major CLIPET

Section CE (counter-intelligence)
Captain WYBOT

November 1943 against 3,472 in July 1944. During the same period, the Intelligence Service sent 1,783 messages.

At the same time, the Gestapo increased its operational tempo as well as the number of arrests. In 1941, 75% of the operations were stopped against 80% in 1942 and 83% in the first half of 1943. On the contrary, the number of operators arrest fell to 15% for the period of July 1943 to July 1944[8], through the adoption of the Electra method. Thus, the Gallia network, that the BCRA had set up in

(continued on page 113)

---

8. Guy Perrier, *Le colonel Passy et les services secrets de la France libre*. Paris, éditions Hachette Littératures, 1999, page 201.

Left.
Bastille day ceremony, 14 July 1943 in London. General Giraud, François d'Astier de la Vigerie and Pierre Fourcaud DSO, OBE, the Commanding Officer of the 1ᵉʳ Bataillon d'Infanterie de l'Air.

Next page.
Even though this is obviously a posed picture, it remains an interesting document as these maquisards are armed with parachuted weapons (M1carbines). The man on the right could be a Jedburgh.
(ECPAD picture)

Pierre Julitte *a.k.a "Robin"*

After some remarkable academics achievements (National Agronomic Institute, the National School of Agricultural Engineering, and the Ecole Supérieure d'Electricité), Pierre Julitte was posted as regimental signal officer in a cavalry unit, the 21st divisional reconnaissance group following the mobilization of August 1939. During the Battle of France, he was put in command of a French liaison mission seconded to the 3rd Armoured Brigade of the British army, under the command of Brigadier General John Crocker. At the end of the campaign, he had received two citations on his Croix de Guerre.

He left France on 18 June to reach England, at the same time as the last British soldiers of the 3rd Brigade. A few days later, he joined the staff of General de Gaulle. He was put in charge of signals. From February 1941, at the request of André Dewavrin, he started working with the BCRA; he was put in charge of covert transmissions with the networks located in France. For this purpose, he was parachuted in France on 11 May 1941, and contributed to the success of the Confrérie Notre-Dame, in the North Zone. In February 1942, his cover was blown and he had to return to London urgently by Lysander. His successes in France during this mission earnt him a third citation

He did not abandon the idea of fighting in France. The Gestapo imprisoned his relatives but he kept on volunteering for further missions inside occupied France. He finally returned on 3 October 1942. After a network infiltration operation led by the Abwehr, he was arrested on 10 March 1943 and imprisoned in the prison of Saint-Pierre (Marseille) then in Fresnes. From there he was deported, on 22 November 1943, first to Neue-Breme and then, on 4 December 1943 to Buchenwald. Far from being demotivated, he continued to provide intelligence reports and to transfer valuable documents regarding the V2 design, which was being developed in Camp Dora, and at the Mibau factory, located in Buchenwald.

These data were considered of strategic importance and contributed to the bombing of the plant and of the deportation camp, on 24 August 1944.

In January 1945, Pierre Julitte was transferred to Camp Dora, and then to Bergen-Belsen in April. British soldiers belonging to the 11th Armored Division released him on 15 April 1945.

His military and covert achievements earnt him a position as a member in the Conseil de l'Ordre de la Libération. Among his decorations were the cross of Commandeur of the Légion d'Honneur, Compagnon de la Libération (Decree of 12 September 1945), the Croix de Guerre 1939/1945 with five citations, the Médaille de la Résistance with Rosette, the Croix du Combattant Volontaire 1939/1945 and the *Médaille Commémorative de la Guerre* 1939-1940. He was also appointed *Commandeur du Mérite Agricole, Commandeur de la Couronne de Chêne Luxembourgeoise* and Member of the British Empire.

(Musée de l'Ordre de la Libération picture)

Top.
Maquisards recovering a CLE Mk I container.

Left.
A day ressuply drop on the col des Saisies pass in the Savoie département on1 August 1944.
(Raymond Bertrand picture)

The Carpetbagger operations

   The B-24 of the 801st/492nd USAAF Bombardment Group flew the "Carpetbaggers" missions from Harrington in Northamptonshire. These nightime, low-altitude missions were flown in support of BCRA, Jedburgh, Sussex and Proust Plans, SOE and OSS operations. The para drops were performed at a very low altitude (190 meters or 600 feet).

   Those special air operations also included the recovery of agents in occupied territory. Between January and September 1944, the 801st/492th bombing group conducted 2,263 missions with a 69% success rate (1,577 successful flights). Between France, Belgium, Holland, and Norway, the Carpetbagger dropped 662 agents, over 18,500 containers and more than 10,700 bundles and recovered 437 individuals.

Pierre Fourcaud
a.k.a "Barbès", "Lucas" and "Sphère"

Russian-by birth and the son of a doctor, son of a doctor, Fourcaud was born in Petrograd (St. Petersburg). Due to the political unrests occurring in Russia, his mother's family immigrated to France and settled in Nice. He was known for his charisma and will power, Dewavrin comparing him to a modern times condottiero.

During the First World War, Fourcaud unlisted and served with the 24th Infantry Regiment. Wounded three times during the Spring and Summer of 1918, he returned to civilian life in 1920 with the rank of Second-Lieutenant. He then joined the 2ᵉ Bureau and conducted a variety of missions thanks to his perfect knowledge of the Russian language.

If his inter-war activities remained unknown, he was mobilized in 1939 with the rank of Captain and joined the 348th Infantry Regiment. He was wounded near Nancy on 16 June 1940. After the armistice, he decided to leave for England and reached Liverpool on 13 July.

Given his language skills - he spoke fluent English, Russian and German- Fourcaud was posted to the Free French intelligence services. He started carrying out operations inside France in 1940, being arrested on 28 August 1941 while trying to persuade French servicemen of the Vichy forces to switch side in favour of general de Gaulle. He managed to escape on 10 August 1942 and reached Gibraltar at the beginning of September passing through the Balearic Islands. He reached London by air and became commander of the 1ᵉʳ Bataillon d'Infanterie de l'Air (1st BIA) at the end of 1942. He was made a Compagnon de la Libération in 1943 (25 May 1943 decree).

At the end of 1943, he returned to France with the task of coordinating the actions of the Savoie maquis. In February 1944, he returned to France under the code-name "Sphère", with the Union Allied mission (January to June 1944), which aimed at providing an update on the needs of the maquis in the Savoie, Isère and Drôme regions. He worked with British SOE Captain Thackthwaite a.k.a "Procureur", and American agent Peter Y. Ortiz, a.k.a "Chambellan" who had been parachuted a few weeks earlier on 7 January 1944. On 19 May 1944, Fourcaud was arrested in Albertville and seriously wounded by two bullets while trying to escape. He survived his wounds and escaped from the Chambery prison on 6 August 1944. He reached London in late August before returning to France on 17 September 1944.

Following the liberation of France, he continued to work for the ecret service as deputy director of the DGER, which quickly became the external service of documentation and counterintelligence (SDECE), a position he held until his retirement in 1956. He was also the founder and director of the Old Comrades association l'*Amicale des Réseaux Action de la France Combattante* and the joint head of the *Comité d'Action de la Résistance* (CAR).

Pierre Fourcaud held many decorations: Croix du Combattant 1914/1918, Croix du Combattant Volontaire 1914/1918, Croix de Guerre 1914/1918 with four citations; Médaille Commémorative 1914/1918; Médaille Interalliée 1914 / 1918, Croix de Guerre 1939/1945 with 5 citations, Médaille de la Résistance with Rosette; Médaille des Evadés. Finally, he received the title of Grand Officer de la Légion d'Honneur. He also awarded numerous foreign decorations: the Distinguished Service Order, Officer of the Order of the British Empire (Great Britain), the Distinguished Service Cross (United States), the title of Commander of the Order of Orange-Nassau (Netherlands), Officer of the Order of Leopold (Belgium) and the Croix de Guerre with Palm (Belgium).

Top.
Pierre Fourcaud, equiped for a refresher jump after the war. At this time, he was the deputy director of the DGER (which then became the SDECE).
(Musée de l'ordre de la Libération picture)

Right.
From top to bottom, clockwise, several different pictures of Pierre Fourcaud at different periods of the war. August 1940 in London, then in the Fort-Barraux jail in November 1941, in August 1942 in the Clermont-Ferrand prison, and finally in September 1942 in Switzerland after having escaped from occupied France.
(François de Rochenoire documents)

Jean Rosenthal a.k.a "Cantinier"

The son of a jeweler, Jean Rosenthal was born in Paris on 5 September 1906. After completing his secondary education at the Ecole Alsacienne he read Law at university. He did his military service in the air force between October 1925 and May 1927 reaching the rank of Sergeant. He then learnt the trade of jeweler with his father until 1935 when he decided to open his own business.

When the war started, he was recalled as a reserve Lieutenant within the *8ᵉ Escadre Aérienne* (8th Air Wing). In July 1940, he was demobilized and he returned to civilian life.

At the end of 1942, he decided to leave France for England through Spain. He reached the United Kingdom on January 23, 1943. The following month, he was assigned to Force "L" with the rank of Lieutenant. He fought as an armoured corps officer under General Leclerc in the Middle east. In July 1943, Leclerc tasked him with a new mission and sent him back to London. There, on 1 September 1943, he joined the BCRA, and, with the rank of Captain and after specialist training, he volunteered to be sent on an operational mission into occupied France under the codename "Cantinier". During the night of 21 to 22 September 1943, with British SOE Colonel Richard Heslop a.k.a "Xavier", he landed by Lysander on the Junot LZ (located in the middle of the Rhône, Ain and Saône-et-Loire départements) in order to carry out Operation Musc. The purpose of this operation was to assess the operational level of the Haute-Savoie maquis and to evaluate their logistics requirements.

They returned to London via a pick-up operation on the night of October 16 to 17, Rosenthal being immediatly debriefed on his mission by General de Gaulle himself. Satisfied with the results, de Gaulle appointed Rosenthal as delegate of Free France and sent him back to occupied France where he landed on the night of 18 to 19 October, near Bletterans (in the Jura département), with three other officers:

Richard Heslop a.k.a "Xavier," U.S. Captain Denis O. Johnson a.k.a, "Paul," a radio operator, and liaison agent Elizabeth Reynolds. One of Rosenthal's cousins, 16 year-old, Micheline Rosenthal a.k.a "Michette", was soon associated to their team as another liaison agent. They all operated from the Haute-Savoie département.

Rosenthal's main task was to prepare for the rise of the French Forces of the Interior while trying to find common grounds with Charles Tillon, the head of the Communist FTP resistance groups.

In 1944, Joseph Rosenthal supported the Glières maquis through a number of resupply drops and engaged in the ill-fated combat operations of March 1944; he also sabotaged the Schmidt-Ross plant in Annecy, which produced ball bearings rendering it unserviceable for months. Finally, he participated in the battles of March 1944, however, that lead to a retreat and lead to a retreat and a dispersion of the guerilla.

On May 3, he did a return trip to London in order to receive some new guidances; he returned to France on the night of 7 to 8 June 1944 by parachute, landing in Cluny (Saône-et-Loire) with Maurice Bourgès and Paul River. From then on his mission was mostly to coordinate and synchronize the actions of the Maquis with the Allied high command.

In August 1944, the résistance liberated Haute-Savoie, capturing nearly 3,000 prisoners in the process. On August 19, 1944, he received, with Major Joseph Lambroschini a.k.a "Nizier", a former member of the Gallia network, the capitulation of the German forces in Haute-Savoie from the hands of German Colonel Meyer.

A few months later, in October, Jean Rosenthal joined the Direction Générale des Etudes et Recherches (Directorate General for Studies and Research or DGER) in order to keep on fighting, this time against the Japanese in the Far East. He returned to France in March 1946 and returned to civilian life in May, taking up once again his occupation as a jeweler. He also became the president of the *Conseil Représentatif des Institutions Juives de France* (Representative Council of Jewish Institutions in France or CRIF) and of the Association Unifiée des Juifs de France (Unified Association of the Jews of France).

Joseph Rosenthal was a Grand Officer of the Legion of Honour and a Compagnon de la Liberation (20 November 1944 decree). He also held the Croix de Guerre 1939-1945 (with 6 citations), the Colonial Medal and the British Military Cross.

Left.
August 1944, liberation of Sallanches in the Haute-Savoie département. On the right, wearing a British uniform, Jean Rosenthal MC a.k.a "Cantinier" and American OSS agent Léon Ball a.k.a "Niveau". The two of them were parachuted on 7 June at 00:30 hours during operation "John 87 A" on the "Metacarpe" dropping zone at Souley near river Arroux in the Gueugnon region of the Saône et Loire département.

Bottom.
Day drop in the Vercors area during the Spring of 1944.
(Musée du Plan Sussex collection)

1943 in conjunction with the MUR, had a real success in terms of intelligence gathering on military and police targets. It had up to 2,500 agents, especially during the Normandy landings phase. Thanks to the good level of operational security maintained by its members, it did not suffer from the German and Vichy French counter intelligence efforts.

Among the other supporting efforts the BCRA could rely on on French soil, Achille Peretti's network, also known as "Ajax" stands out. Created in June 1943, it was mosty composed of policemen coming from the Ali network[9]. From its "headquarters" located in Lyon, it participated in the intelligence gathering efforts as well as to the exfiltration of compromised agents, resistants and Jews. Thanks to its sub-networks, the expanse of Ajax was very important: its structure extended into Spain, Switzerland and Italy.

Overall, it fielded 1,189 agents, 29 of whom died (11 in deportation, 18 were killed or shot). Between 1942 and 1944, nearly two dozen intelligence networks operated on French soil. Their activities reflected the ever-increasing collection and transfer of intelligence reports to London. The "Military Mail" section of the BCRA created on 15 March 1943 sorted the messages and plans.

This section was firstly directed by Jean Pierre-Bloch (1905-1999), who came from the SOE, then

9. The Ali or Caviar network (named after its cofounder Paul Joly a.k.a "Caviar") was one of the five franco-belgian networks to have existed during the Second World War. The others were: Zéro-France, PCB-PCC, Sabot and Delbo-Phénix. The Ali II network was established by the belgian state security services in exile in London and it operated in France as a relay between the Belgian networks and the Belgian, Portuguese and Spanish intelligence services. The name is the alias chosen by its main founder Joseph Dubar a.k.a Jean du Nord or Jean de Roubaix, the city of his origins.

Top.
Colonel Romans-Petit DSO, commander of the Ain département maquis, and British SOE Colonel Richard Heslop DSO a.k.a "Xavier" in the Ain in 1944.

Left.
British SOE Colonel Richard Heslop DSO a.k.a "Xavier" belonged to the " Musc " mission (September-October 1943). The aim of this mission, which also included Jean Rosenthal from the BCRA was to evaluate the status of the Haute-Savoie maquis, to gauge their logistic requirements, their personnel strength and their operational capability.
(Musée du Plan Sussex collection)

Stéphane Hessel

In 1917 in Berlin, Stéphane Hessel was born in a family of Jewish tradition that immigrated to France where he was naturalized in 1937.

After his High Scool diploma in Philosophy obtained in June 1933, he studied at the London School of Economics and at the Free School of Political Science. He passed the examination at the Ecole Normale in 1937, that he was forced to take again in 1939, having become French in 1937.

At the time of the Battle of France he served in a cyclists company, in the Sarre area, and was taken prisoner at Saint-Dié (Vosges), and interned in a camp at Bourbonne-les-Bains (Haute-Marne). He escaped from the camp and decided to join the Free French. He asked to be demobilized and reached England via Lisbon and Oran in March 1941, to join the FFL. After a long stay at the Patriotic School, he served from March 1942 as a navigator in the Air Force.

In 1943, he met Tony Mella, the son of the hotel Ritz owner, who facilitated his joining the BCRA, first as a liaison agent with the British and then as a member of the R section of which he quickly became one of the leading elements. His task was to ensure a smooth relationship between the staff and the internal resistance. However, he also participated to an operation in France in March 1944 (Mission Gréco); his mission was to set up reporting sites in order to prepare for the forthcoming landing operations.

He was quickly arrested in July 1944 and deported in early August, as a secret agent, to the Buchenwald camp; he owed his life to a substitution of identity with another Frenchman, Michel Boitel, who had died of typhus on the day he was supposed to be executed. He managed to be transferred in October 1944 to a landing gear factory in Rottleberode. Following an escape attempt, he was sent to the Dora camp from where he managed to escape during a transfer to the camp of Bergen-Belsen in April 1945.

At the end of the war, he joined the Ministry of Foreign Affairs and began a career as diplomat first in China and then in the United Nations headquarters in New York, as secretary of the commission in charge of drafting of the Charter of the Human rights of 1948.

Stéphane Hessel was awarded the Grand-Croix de l'Ordre national du Mérite in 1999 and was made a Grand Officier de l'Ordre National de la Légion d'Honneur in 2006.

Top.
Maquisards getting ready to destroy the containers they have just emptied of their precious loads.

Top.
London 1943, Stéphane Hessel.
(National Archives picture)

by Gilbert Renault, a.k.a "Rémy" or "Roulier"[10]. It centralized the messages that were then typed and distributed to the different recipients.

However, it did not stop missions involving British and French agents of the BCRA from being deployed on operation. In September 1943, Mission "Musc" was composed of Jean Rosenthal a.k.a "Cantinier" as radio operator for the BCRA, and British Colonel Richard Harry Heslop a.k.a "Xavier", who belonged to the SOE. On the night of 21 to 22 September 1943, a twin engined Hudson dropped

them on the "Junot" DZ near Pont-de-Vaux. Their mission was to assess the equipment, weapons and logistics needs of the Haute-Savoie résistance groups. Rosenthal emitted from the Gendarmerie buildings in Megève. The team was recovered during a pickup operation on the night of 16 to 17 October, near Manziat. During their London stay, thanks to the study of their report an Allied mission was sent in order to support and enable the rise of the Haute-Savoie maquis. Jean Rosenthal also took part in that mission. He returned to the Ain department and

(continued on page 119)

Top and bottom.
A ceremony in Milton Hall, the Jedburgh School. At the end of their training cycle, which was dedicated to unconventional warfare and covert operations, the agents from the different nations were integrated into multinational teams before being parachuted in occupied France.
(National Archives pictures)

10. Jean-Pierre Bloch was appointed Deputy Commissioner of the Interior Ministry in Algiers.

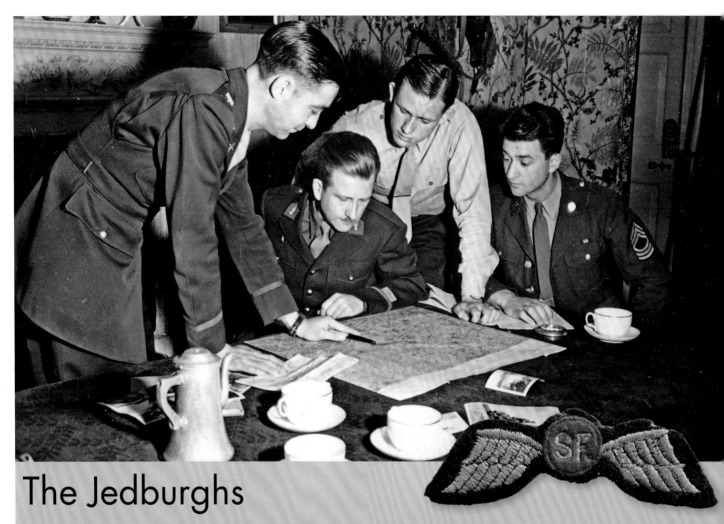

The Jedburghs

Top.
A Jedburgh team studies the map of its future area of operations in the Spring of 1944.
(National Archives picture)

The Jedburgh plan concept was devised by the SOE (Special Operations Executive) in July 1942. The OSS (Office of Strategic Services), understanding the value of Résistance movements and taking into account the experience of the SOE then established contacts with the British service before the North Africa landings in order to analyse the possibility of sending teams in occupied territories tasked with the facilitation of the advance of conventional forces. Unfortunately, those early contacts did not produce much so, in order to get a reaction from the high command, the SOE organised exercise Spartan

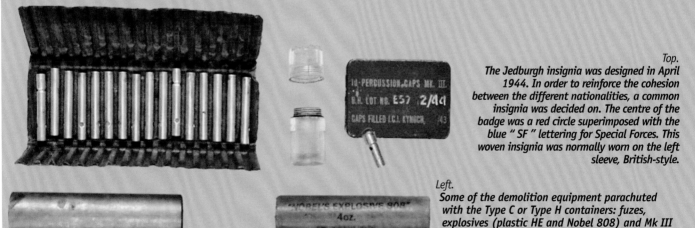

Top.
The Jedburgh insignia was designed in April 1944. In order to reinforce the cohesion between the different nationalities, a common insignia was decided on. The centre of the badge was a red circle superimposed with the blue " SF " lettering for Special Forces. This woven insignia was normally worn on the left sleeve, British-style.

Left.
Some of the demolition equipment parachuted with the Type C or Type H containers: fuzes, explosives (plastic HE and Nobel 808) and Mk III priming charges.
(Frédéric Vemon collection)

116

from the 3 to the 11 March 1943. The Americans came as observers. The after action report was so positive that five days latter a joint memo was drafted by the OSS and SOE. The roles were defined as well as the command and control structures; manpower was set at 70 3-man teams including one from the nation were the team was to operate ; the tasks when operating with the maquis and the communication systems were also detailed. The decision was taken to parachute teams in military uniforms but civilian clothes were also deemed acceptable. In April, the total number of teams was grown to 100, including 30 provided by occupied nations (France, Belgium, Holland) because the planners anticipated heavy casualties.

TRAINING AT ME 65

The training cycle of the Jedburgh teams mainly took place between April and December 1943 at Military Establishment 25 or ME 65 (the Jedburgh Training School) located on the Milton Hall camp in Cambridgeshire. An expert in guerilla techniques, Lieutenant-Colonel George Richard Musgrave who had served under Wingate, led this school. The training was particularly advanced and the operators were thoroughly tested, both psychologicaly and physicaly. Their technical skills and knowledge were also the subject of a ruthless selection. Exercises were conducted under realistic conditions, usually at night and with live ammunition.

In August 1943, BCRA Major Maurice Duclos a.k.a "Saint-Jacques" made a famous speech to the hundred of French in training / selection for the Jedburgh program: "you'll be the first to fight on French soil, but you will pay dearly for this privilege because in a few weeks 75% of you will die in combat. Those who will survive will have no special rights or bonuses or decorations, or promotions, or glory. For those who will be killed, they will die anonymously and completely alone. They will, under torture, experience sheer terror and a slow and ignominious death, and nobody will ever know where, when or how they died."

During the specialist training (which lasted about six months), emphasis was put on demolition techniques (railways, tunnels, bridges, roads, buildings), sabotage, guerrilla, unarmed combat, escape and evasion and communication and encryption techniques. All the Jedburghs were also parachute trained, having performed five jumps at the Ringway School, including two from a balloon.

THE MISSIONS

From 6 June 1944, the missions took off from Tempsford and Harrington when leaving from the UK and from Maison Blanche and Blida when leaving from French North Africa.

The missions were active in five areas: Brittany; the Loire valley ; the Châteauroux-Toulouse axis ; the Alps and the South-East of France ; and finally, the North-East. In June, the main objective was to slow down the German reinforcements that were heading towards Normandy; then, in the following months, the teams were mostly tasked with the protection of the flanks of the advancing allied armies advancing from Normandy and Provence. Both missions were carried out successfully.

Jedburgh teams were deployed as such: in June 13 teams were dropped in the South and Centre of France as well as in Brittany. In July, another 11 were dispatched to Brittany and the Centre-West of France. In August, following the landings in Provence, support to the maquis intensified and

53 teams were parachuted in the South West of France and in the Alps. In September 10 teams reinforced the East of France. On the Atlantic front, 4 other teams had a maritime insertion. In November, one last team was sent to Alsace to face a possible German counter-attack. Each team jumped with a dozen weapons containers; this allowed the Jedburghs to start training the maquis while waiting for further weapons drops requested through their own communication systems. Direct command of the maquis was not automatic and depended on circumstances but supervision was the norm.

THE JEDBURHS : AN ASSESSMENT

In total, of 92 Jedburghs teams were deployed in France including one close to the Belgium border. Another 8 teams were dropped in Holland, including 6 in support of Operation Market Garden.

285 men were qualified as Jedburghs (103 French, 89 British, 83 Americans, 8 Dutch, 1 Belgian and 1 Canadian). The grim predictions of a rate loss of 40 % and over luckily were proven wrong by facts. Nevertheless, 19 Jedburghs were killed (13 in action, 4 shot after capture and 2 fatal parachuting accidents); 25 were wounded or injured (18 in action and 7 in parachute accidents) and four were taken as 4 prisoners of war.

Bertrand SOUQUET

Top.
The parachute tower at Ringway as used by OSS, SOE and BCRA agents during their Jedburgh training at Milton Hall.
(National Archives picture)

Top.
On Lyon' place Bellecour, on 5 September 1944, Jedburgh Jean Larrieu, who had received an Army level citation for his actions during the combat operations of the Summer of 1944 receives the Croix de Guerre with palm.
(Larrieu family picture)

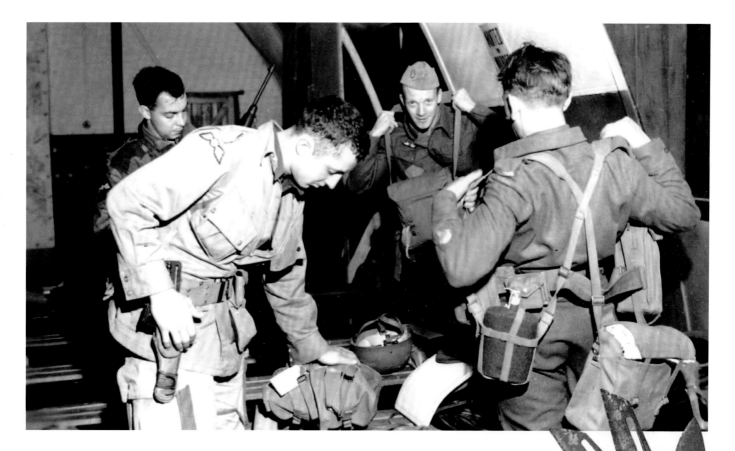

was infiltrated near Bletterans (Jura), on the night of October 18 to 19 1943, with Elizabeth Reynolds, a.k.a "Rochester", and Owen Denis Johnson, a member of the OSS, who was a radio Operator[11].

Despite the operational needs, the air operations and arms deliveries in support of the BCRA in France remained rare. For the first nine months of 1943, 19 landings (including pick-up operations tasked with the exfiltration of compromised agents) and 72 para drops were conducted in support of the BCRA[12]. On the contrary, during Autumn 1943 - (as during the Winter of 1943-1944), the weather was largely unfavorable for airdrops. Climatic hazards heavily weighed on the conduct of guerrilla warfare, as the needs for both weapons and equipment were becoming increasingly important, as the maquis grew in strength.

For example, all the airdrops operations planned for December 1942 were cancelled because of bad weather. In January 1943, only 13 of the 35 planned airdrops took place. In September 1943,

Previous page.
On 11 August 1944, on RAF Harrington, pre-jump checks for the "Anis" mission before boarding the B-24 which will soon drop them over France. On the right, Cécile Pichard who has already completed her checks looks at Maurice Rosbach, a.k.a "Sévillan", the mission's radio operator, who is filling his pockets with banknotes. "Anis" was parachuted over DZ "Hôtel" near Rivière-les-Fosses in the Haute-Marne département during the night of the 11 to the 12 of August 1944.
(National Archives picture)

Top.
The "Ronald" Jedburgh team loading up before boarding the plane which would soon parachute them at 03:09 hours on 5 August 1944 in the Vannes region. Left to right: two American operators, Sergeant Elmer B. Esch and Second Lieutenant Shirly Ray Trumps and two French officers, Lieutenant Georges Deseilligny and Second Lieutenant Dumas, the radio operator of the "Aloes" mission.
(National Archives picture)

Right.
The escape and evasion SOE knife attached to the jump suit. Additional informations on this knife can be found on page 74 of Clandestine Parachute and Pick-up Operations by Jean-Louis Perquin Editions H&C.
(Jean-Thomas Duclos collection)

---

11. The team was led by Richard Heslop and was composed of an OSS radio officer, Owen Denis Johnson a.k.a "Paul," Elisabeth Reynolds, a.k.a "Rochester" and Jean Rosenthal from the BCRA.
12. Guy Perrier, *Le colonel Passy et les services secrets de la France libre. Op. cit.*, page 197.

The Sussex plan
Special teams and a special squadron

SUSSEX 1944

Following a decision of the SHAEF in March 1943, it was decided to launch the Sussex plan. The idea was to send two-man teams (two officers, an observer and a radio operator) in the French regions located North of the river Loire) in order to carry out combined military intelligence gathering missions without relying on the Résistance networks.

The BCRA was in charge of recruitment and formation of these teams, with the agreement of the OSS and IS. Recruitment was overseen by Colonels Rémy (Gilbert Renault) and Saint-Jacques (Maurice Duclos). It took place between the Summer of 1943 and February 1944.

120 volunteers were selected, including two women (Jeanne Guyot, called "Jeannette" and Evelyne Clopet a.k.a "Chamonnet"). Only four of the 118 men were more than 30, the others being aged 17 to 26.

Most of them were selected in North Africa and sent to England for a new series of tests before attending specialized training (six to three months depending on their arrival date). The training was given in Saint Albans, in OSS and IS schools (Praewood House), some 40 kilometers North of London. Covert operations and direct action techniques were taught. The whole site was under the responsibility of British Colonel Malcolm Henderson and American Colonel Neave. British commandos and U.S. Marines, under the command of Captain Guy Wingate, provided the education and training. The future agents were also given parachute training at the British parachute school of Ringway, near Manchester. Wingate created the specific badge of the Sussex agents, on which three national flags can be seen, symbolizing the participation of the BCRA, OSS and IS, just below the title

Sussex 1944. The badge was produced and distributed after the liberation of Paris.

The OSS trained 26 teams in Grendon, against 28 for the IS.The teams parachuted into France from Liberators or Halifax. They had specific ultra high frequency (UHF) transmitters called the S-Phone (Mark 7, of English manufacture, or TR1 of American design), which allowed communications between a ground operator and a crewmember in a plane.

This is why a specialized squadron was established: the Sussex Squadron, flying B25 Mitchell, and placed under the command of Squadron Leader Winney. The Sussex Squadron was based on Hartflordbridge camp and was part of 226 Squadron.

If the Squadron pilots were British, the nine radio operators and observers were French, including the famous writer Joseph Kessel and André Bernheim.

On the ground, the agents were giving intelligence on German troop movements and depots. Overall, it is estimated that they sent more than 700 messages, that over 500 were processed and that they led to bombings of strategic importance. During their 54 officially established missions, they were able to create as many local networks, each with an average of 5 to 10 members, mainly located in the northern half of France.

When Operation Overlord was launched, the Proust plan was added to the Sussex plan in order to increase the number of agents in the field by adding another eight teams (16 agents on the sixty trained for this purpose). They were tasked with gathering intelligence on the rear of the German lines.

The Allies were unanimous about the importance of the Sussex program and its results.

Beyond the Allied operations inherent to the Normandy landing, a dozen Sussex agents and a member of the BCRA joined the Target Force, which was in charge of seizing the Abwehr archives during the liberation of Paris before they were destroyed by the Germans themselves. The "Sussex Normandy", was thus attached to the Free French 2nd Armoured Division and it went to the Majestic Hotel on 23 August 1944. In the French capital, the BCRA agents, including those related to the Sussex plan, had safe heavens such as the Café located 8 rue Tournefort in the 5th arrondissement held by Andrée Goubillon.

Of the 120 Sussex agents, 101 parachuted into occupied France and nine were killed by the Germans, including Evelyne Clopet.

Previous page, center.
The insignia of the Plan Sussex. Over a modern French shield, a parachute holding a cross of Lorraine superimposed on a French flag with, on each side, a British and an American flag. On top, " Sussex 1944 " on black enamel. The three national flags represent the BCRA (France), the OSS (United States) and the MIS (British). The cross of Lorraine is a reminder that BCRA agents were part of the Fighting French and the black enamel that the agents arrived on French soil by night.
(Private collection, Jean-Louis Perquin picture)

only 27 operations were carried out, 14 in October and 8 in December 1943. As for containers, their number, for the same periods decreased from 225 in September to 160 in October and about 50 in December. The BCRA never ceased to request more and more equipment [13].

1944 : PRIORITY IS GIVEN TO DIRECT ACTION MISSIONS

By 1944, the flow of intelligence reports reaching London from France was continuous. The Operation section received a daily average of 6.2 messages during the first half of 1943, against 17.1 in the second half of the same year, 70.5 in the Spring of 1944 and 120.5 by May 1944 [14]. The volume of reports sent covertly from France to the BCRA was close to 1,000 a day; on top of that, on average over 2,000 plans were also received every week.

In preparation for the Normandy landings, 1944 saw a significant increase in the number of parachute drop operations. Compared to 1943, shipments of

13. Sébastien Albertelli, *Les Services secrets du Général de Gaulle. Le BCRA 1940-1944.* Paris, éditions Perrin, 2010, page 439.
14. Sébastien Albertelli, *op. cit.,* page 391.

Top.
French Captain William Bechtel MC a.k.a "Louis Bonnet" of the mission Berthier (Brissex) was parachuted on 9 April 1944 over Neuvy-Pailloux in the Indre. The team would operate in the Rouen region and took part in the liberation of the city of Rouen itself.
(Musée du Plan Sussex picture)

Pierre Rateau
a.k.a "Henri Poily", "Pape", "Arthur", "Eminence", "Rossi"

He was one of the 180 Frenchmen (nicknamed "the Russians") who had escaped from German POW camps through Russia and who, under the command of Pierre Billotte had finally reached the UK. Posted to the BCRA, he was trained by the Intelligence Service. In April 1943, Second Lieutenant Rateau was parachuted in occupied France near Roanne in the Loire département under the code name "Arthur". He was put in charge of the *Service des Atterrissages et Parachutages* (Landing and Parachute Operations Service) for the R3 and R4 regions (Toulouse and Montpellier). He settled in Toulouse from where he organised his service which had by then changed name to become the *Section des Atterrissages et des Parachutages* (Landing and Parachute Operations Section or SAP). He thus was in charge of the reception committees of the first air operations in the South-West of France and was responsible for the safe circulation between France and the UK of some of the key players of Free France such as Pierre Brossolette, Pierre Viénot, Jules Moch or Henri Queuille.

Tracked by the Gestapo, he had several narrow escapes. He also organised a rat line towards Spain which helped several BCRA agents to cross the border. In February 1944, he used this itinerary to return to London where he arrived in April. Posted to General Koenig's staff, he was put in charge of air liaisons with the operation officers and the network commanders. In August 1944, he was parachuted a second time into France (mission Shinoil) on the Saint-Nazaire pocket in order to gather the *maquis* of the Vendée region. On completion, he was appointed as head of the *4e Bureau*. Pierre Rateau received the Croix de la Libération from the hands of General de Gaulle on 18 June 1945 before being posted to the Direction Générale des Etudes et Recherches (DGER). He was demobilised during the Summer of 1945.

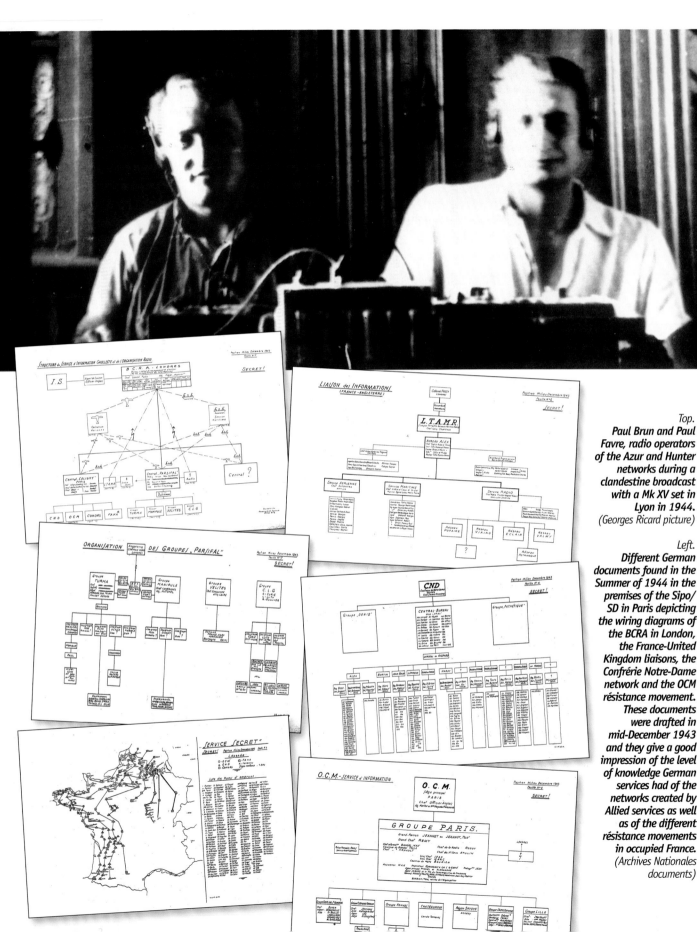

Top.
Paul Brun and Paul Favre, radio operators of the Azur and Hunter networks during a clandestine broadcast with a Mk XV set in Lyon in 1944.
(Georges Ricard picture)

Left.
Different German documents found in the Summer of 1944 in the premises of the Sipo/SD in Paris depicting the wiring diagrams of the BCRA in London, the France-United Kingdom liaisons, the Confrérie Notre-Dame network and the OCM résistance movement.
These documents were drafted in mid-December 1943 and they give a good impression of the level of knowledge German services had of the networks created by Allied services as well as of the different résistance movements in occupied France.
(Archives Nationales documents)

explosives were increased by a factor of 7, increasing from 74 to 518 tonnes. Drops of sub machine guns increased from 28,000 to 169,000 units[15].

In 1943, the BCRA had only received 7,387 sub-machine guns, 5,278 pistols and 12 rifles[16]... In contrast, in 1944, nearly 55% of the containers drops were then made in support of the BCRA in anticipation of the landing. These figures were the direct results of a series of meeting between Emmanuel d'Astier de La Vigerie and Churchill, between January and February 1944.

THE IMPORTANCE OF AIR SUPPORT

In early 1944, most of the air operations were performed by the Royal Air Force, as the United States Army Air Forces (USAAF) – and especially the "Carpetbaggers" Squadron – were dedicated to bombing operations. From March 1944, the situation evolved when the Supreme Headquarters Allied Expeditionary Forces (SHAEF) took control of all secret services activities in connection with

15. *Ibid.*, page 410.
16. Jean-Louis Crémieux-Brilhac, *La France libre. De l'appel du 18 juin à la Libération.* Paris, éditions Gallimard, 1996, page 772.

Top.
Operating the S-Phone on the ground and from a flying aircraft.
(Now it can be told picture)

Right.
The MCR 1 " Biscuit " receiver got that nickname because it was delivered in a biscuit box. Designed during the second half of the war, the "Biscuit" was a high sensitivity, five miniature valve superheterodyn covering 150Khz to 15Mhz with an IF of 1.73Mhz. When the MCR 1 was initially delivered, it was considered as a technical marvel. 10,000 of those sets were producedand about half of those were parachuted in 1944, almost one for each operational landing site. This widespread distribution found its origin in the assessment that, because of air raids or sabotage operations, the main power supply would likely be cut during the period comprized between the D-day and the Liberation. This in turn meant that the reception committees would not be able to listen to the BBC broadcasts that always preceded parachute and landing operations.
(IWM picture)

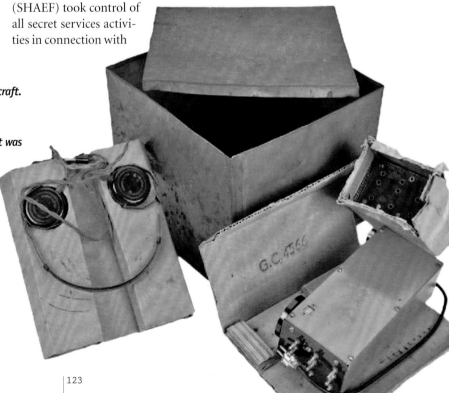

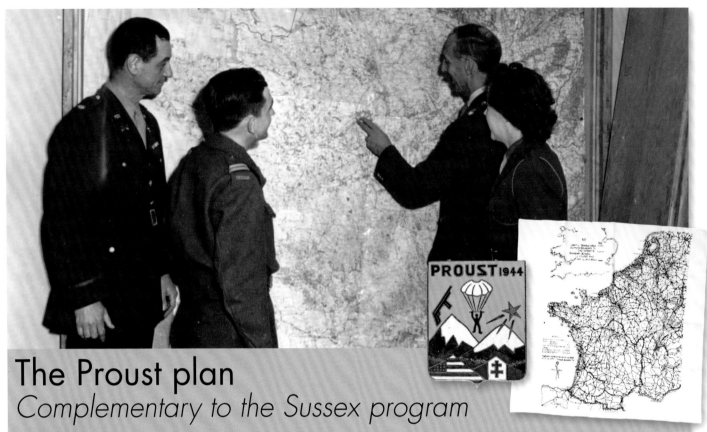

The Proust plan
Complementary to the Sussex program

Under the responsibility of U.S. Colonel Neave and his French deputy, Major Dutey, the Proust program was launched in January 1944. It was envisioned as a complement to the actions of the Sussex plan. The name Proust (a famous French writer) was chosen by OSS Colonel Justin O'Brien who oversaw the training of the two plans. In civilian life, Justin O'Brien was a professor teaching French littrature at Columbia University

The Proust plan was staffed with personnel considered as surplus to the Sussex plan as well as BCRA elements from North Africa as confirmed by a memo # 379D/BCRAL from the BCRA London Office to the BCRAL Algiers Office dated 11 February 1944.

Thus Proust consisted of a series of intelligence gathering missions conducted in France in support of the U.S. Staff after the Normandy landing These missions were considered as complementary to the Sussex plan operations. Initially, Proust provided for the use of fifty French and American agents behind enemy lines.

From March 1944, the volunteers were trained by the OSS in Drungwick Manor (code name Area B), in Horsham. Training was entrusted to Lieutenant-Colonel Waller B. Booth from the OSS. It was identical to the training given to Sussex officers. The preparation of the Proust plan suffered from a lack of resources as the logistics priority was given to the Sussex plan. In addition, the selection of candidates reduced the number of potential agents to sixty-five (in May 1944) and then to fifty.

Most of the teams were dropped into France; only two teams had a maritime insertion and another two were flown in. During the first mission called "Girafe" (launched 25 June 1944), Joseph Michel Jourden alias "Jean-Marie Stur" was killed at Plouigneau, in the area of Morlaix, on 9 August 1944. He was to be Proust's only casualty. In August, some Proust officers were detached to the 3rd and 7th American Armies for intelligence and reconnaissance missions. Subsequently, many of them were integrated into the DGER.

Top and top à right.
In the Spring of 1944, members of a Jedburgh team which includes a French officer are briefed on their future area of operations in France by one of the commanders of the Jedburgh Plan.
(National Archives picture)

Left.
During the Summer of 1944, BCRA teams leading maquisards groups managed to seize several French cities in the face of strong German opposition. On this picture, a French BCRA officer belonging to a Jedburgh team.
(25e DIM picture)

Top center.
The insignia of the Plan Proust, which was produced in 1945 for its agents. It bears the following elements: a paratrooper armed with a submachine gun descends on snow capped mountains surrounded by barbed wires, the symbol of occupied and enslaved nations...the French and American flags are reminders of the two nations that took part in this plan, which, unlike Sussex, did not comprize any British element.
(Private collection, Jean-Louis Perquin picture)

Operation Overlord. From 1 May 1944, the Special Forces Headquarters (SFHQ) was created. It was placed in command of all the operations carried out by both the SOE and the OSS, in coordination with the BCRA. General Pierre Koenig, (military delegate of the French Committee of National Liberation (CFLN) and senior commander of the French forces in Great-Britain, and then in May, military delegate to the North Zone operations) made certain, via a specific staff element assigned to Colonel Vernon, that the French and Allied special operations were both synchronized and coordinated with the operations of the internal resistance, in anticipation of the landings. This point gave rise to the formation of a FFI-Staff (EM-FFI), which was put under SHAEF command from July 1944.

Until May 1944, the Americans only dedicated a few airframes to support covert operations (14 aircraft, compared to 84 for the RAF). From 26 May 1944, the

Top.
Members of the Corps Franc Pommiès (CFP) entering the city of Tarbes, which was liberated on 24 August 1944. The CFP, under the command of Captain André Pommiés was activated after the Vichy Armistice Army was disbanded in 1942. Between 1942 and 1944, the CFP carried out the sabotage of 12 factories, 7 high voltage lines, 40 steam locomotives and eliminated 68 agents and officers of the Gestapo and Sipo-SD. Trained and equipped by Jedburgh teams, the 8,000-man strong CFP, including 6,000 armed men, took part in the liberation of the cities of Tarbes, Pau as well as a large part of the South-West of France.
(François de Rochenoire collection picture)

André Pelabon

Born in the North of France, in Vieux-Condé, André Pelabon graduated from the prestigious Ecole Polytechnique (class of 1928), before training as a maritime and aeronautical engineer. He also graduated in 1936 from the School of Oriental Languages. In June 1940, he was assigned to the Aeronautical Department of the Navy, and as such, tasked with the establishment of a network of secret deposits of raw materials and machinery in Morocco.

By 1941, Pelabon had a close relationship with the U.S. consular service in Casablanca to which he communicated a lot of intelligence reports on the situation in Morocco. Thanks to the Americans and passing through Gibraltar, he managed to reach England and to join the Free French in London in August 1942.

Between February 1943 and October 1943, André Pelabon was assigned to the logistics corps of the Navy, before being appointed to the personal staff of General de Gaulle in Algiers, a position he held from October 1943 to September 1944. Among his tasks was the direction of the BCRA office in Algiers ... During these activities on behalf of the BCRA, it is likely that he collaborated with with Jean Moulin.

From the end of World War II, he led the career of a high-ranking civil servant, especially within the Ministry of Interior.

André Pelabon was appointed Commander of the Légion d'Honneur, Commander of the British Empire and Commander of the Order of Leopold II. He was also the holder of the Croix de guerre 1939-1945 and the Médaille de la Résistance with Rosette.

USAAF added another two squadrons of Liberator to this effort. From then on, 115 bombers adapted to special operation and another fifteen aircrafts dedicated to covert landings were earmarked for the support of the secret services.

Between January and September 1944, about 7,000 air missions were conducted, half in support of the SOE and OSS, 9% of the SAS, 8% of the Algiers Special Operations Centre (SPOC) and 37% in favor of the BCRA. From July to the end of September 1944, more than 50,000 containers were parachuted into France including 3,690 tons of weapons for August only [17].

In 1943, the planning section of BCRA adopted color codes depending on the nature of the missions planned for the beginning of 1944. The destruction of power plants was given the colour blue. Railways and rolling stock sabotage were green. These operations were mainly conducted by SNCF (the French railway company) agents themselves. The destruction of ammunition and weapon depots were yellow. Red was for missions on fuel depots, while the " Plans Tortue " (Turtle plans) – to be renamed Bibendum - focused on the road network in order to disrupt, slow or paralyze the movement of German units. Finally, the purple plans dealt with the communication networks and the long distances underground transmission lines.

SHAEF only agreed to activate these plans on 20 April 1944. By sea or air, the direct action teams performed demolition missions, targeting power plants, German army radio stations or Nazi command posts. Harassment, routes denial and guerrilla actions are carried out against the enemy... These missions were mostly assigned to teams and guerrilla forces that could fall back on natural safe heavens for protection such as the Pyrenees, the Massif Central, the Alps, the Jura, the Vosges and the Morvan as well as some other locations in Brittany and in the Indre département.

On 16 May 1944, de Gaulle signed, an " instruction concernant l'emploi de la Résistance sur le plan militaire au cours des opérations de Libération " (orders on the use of the resistance for military matters during Liberation operations"). At this stage, and contrarily to his position of 1943, de Gaulle no longer seemed to be in favour of a national insurrection in order to avoid an indiscriminate German crackdown. Within the Free French decision circles, this decision was seen as controversial.

Finally, on Eisenhower's decision, (but in total contradiction with the wishes of Charles de Gaulle) the SOE launched the operations it had been planning for months on 1 June 1944. The French résistance networks were put on the alert by 160 BBC messages. On 5 June at 9:15 pm, the SOE received confirmation that the landings would take place in the forthcoming 48 hours. This triggered a series of operations by the Résistance; 80% of the

(continued on page 130)

17. Jean-Louis Crémieux-Brilhac, *La France libre. De l'appel du 18 juin à la Libération.* Paris, éditions Gallimard, 1996, page 866.866.

Bottom.
A Type C container.
(IWM picture)

Bottom.
Recovering containers after a day resupply drop on 1 August 1944 on the Glières plateau.

Weapons for the Résistance

According to Colonel Maurice J. Buckmaster, head of SOE F, 418,083 weapons were delivered to the French Résistance. Of those weapons, 47 % were submachine guns (mostly Sten), 30 % were rifles (mostly of the british Lee-Enfield type), 14 % were handguns (57,849 pistols and revolvers), 5 % were light machineguns (mostly Bren), 2 % were US M1 carbines and 1 % were antitank weapons.

Left.
On the left, holding a bouquet, aspirant Marcel Charles a.k.a "Péroné" of the BCRA. He was parachuted on 10 September 1944 near Chamblay, in the vicinity of the city of Dôle in the Franche- Comté region as part of operation "Bob 285".

Bottom.
The south zone was divided into 6 regions numbered between 1 and 6. The North Zone also comprized 6 regions but it used letters as reference: A, B (2 sub-regions), C, D (2 sub-regions), M (2 sub-regions), P (2 sub-regions).

The Regional Military Delegates (DMR)

From September 1943 on, the délégués militaires régionaux (DMR) were officers who were either sent or appointed by the BCRA in order to operate inside metropolitan France (i.e not in French colonies such as Algeria for example). There were twelve DMRs and their areas of responsability were in line with Jean Moulin and Henry Frenay's guidelines.

The Regional Military Delegates were placed under the authority of the Zone delegates: North Zone (occupied zone) or South (the former non-occupied zone). The Zone delegates answered to a national delegate. During the war, the national delegates were Pierre Marchal a.k.a Hussard, Louis Mangin a.k.a Losange, Maurice Bourgès-Maunoury and Jacques Chaban-Delmas.

The hierarchical authority of the DMR was the BCRA. Several regions were divided into sub-sectors, both in the West of France and in the Paris region.

The main responsibility of the Regional Military Delegates was to enforce the different colour-coded plans that were devised in London in anticipation for the Allied landings.

Initially, the DMRs were envisioned as representatives of London sent as ambassadors or technical advisors to the Résistance movements and they were not supposed to have any command responsibilities. After a while, and even though their authority was often resented by local résistance groups, they became a vital coordination element which even managed to synchronize operations with the Communist résistance movements. Sometimes, FFI leaders were appointed as DMRs such as Gilbert Grandval in region C (city of Châlons-sur-Marne).

The DMR role was also very important when it came to disseminating intelligence and information and when limited assets had to be shared between different groups. Since they had direct access to the BCRA in London through their own radio sets, their power was considerable.

Considering the multiplicity of tasks the DMRs had top perform, they were soon seconded by officers of the *Centre d'Opérations de Parachutages et d'Atterrissages* (COPA, Landing and Parachute Operations Center) and then by members of the *Section des Atterrissages et des Parachutages* (SAP, Landing and Parachute Operations Section). They were tasked with the reconnaissance and selection of both landing and dropping zones and with the coordination of deliveries.

The DMRs were all supporters of General de Gaulle; these officers were also all volunteers, they had followed commando-type training and their average age was thirty. Their life expectancy, once inside occupied France in areas they often did not know intimately, was no more than five months.

The first DMRs were infiltrated inside occupied France during the night of 11 to 12 September 1943 on a landing zone near the city of Tours in support of operations in the North zone. The dangerous work of the DMRs received little publicity but no less than eleven Regional Military Delegates eventually became Compagnon de la Libération.

André Boulloche

Born on 7 September 1915 in Paris, André Boulloche spent the 1939-1940 period first as a reserve officer in an engineer unit and was then transferred to the Air Force. On 24 June 1940, he made his way to French North Africa in order to keep on fighting and then tried unsuccessfully to reach London. On his return to France, he was asked by Postel-Vinay to organize an intelligence gathering network in the Aisne département. When Postel-Vinay was arrested at the end of December 1941, André Boulloche took control of the network for the North region. During 1942, the network spread and started operating in the whole of the occupied zone. On top of his intelligence gathering tasks, André Boulloche established contacts with the leaders of the *Armée Secrète* (AS) and started organising the military infrastructure of the Résistance.

Hunted down by the Gestapo, he crossed the Spanish border on 25 December 1942 and finally reached the United Kingdom in May 1943. Volunteering to return to occupied France, André Boulloche was landed by a Lysander on 13 September 1943, as the Military Delegate of the Region P (Paris). With the leaders of the *Armée Secrète,* under the alias of "Armand", he established the paramilitary structures of the Résistance while, at the same time, organizing many sabotage operations on behalf of the Allied command.

Arrested in his house by the Gestapo on 12 January 1944, he tried to escape but was shot and severely wounded. Treated at the Hôpital de la Pitié in Paris, he was then transferred to the Fresnes prison. Deported to Auschwitz, then Buchenwald and finally Flossenburg, André Boulloche was freed on 23 April 1945. His father, mother and brother, who had all been arrested in August 1944, never returned from German concentration camps.

Eugène Déchelette

Born on 5 January 1906 in the city of Roanne. Fought as a reserve officer with the 216 Infantry Regiment in Lorraine, Belgium and Holland. Taken prisoner in Lille, he managed to escape and to reach London on 31 July 1940.

First posted to the General de Gaulle's staff, he then joined the BCRA in June 1941. In August 1941, he was posted to the 2e bureau of Thierry d'Argenlieu's staff in the Pacific.

After this mission, he returned to London in June 1943 and was posted again to the BCRA. He volunteered for a mission in occupied France and after extensive training was parachuted on 29 January 1944 in the Drôme département in order to take the position of Regional Military Delegate for the R5 Region (city of Limoges) with the nom-de-guerre of "Ellipse". Breaking his right ankle on landing, Eugène Déchelette nevertheless circulated around his area of responsibility in order to establish contact with the different résistance groups and to apportion on the assets under his control. Showing good diplomatic skills, he managed to appease the tensions between the different movements, coordinating the operations and appointing FFI commanders as needed. Finally, he organized the R5 Action network. His deputy was Gérard Hennebert a.k.a "Baron", who was the regional air operations commander and by George Héritier a.k.a "Croc" who became his executive officer during the Spring of 1944.

Eugène Déchelette's support to the résistance movements proved crucial after the June 1944 landings, especially when the maquis were facing German armoured units trying to reach Normandy.

Between geometrical figures, ecclesiastical or nobility titles, farming tools and ancient names…

The DMR used the names of geometrical figures as aliases ; Carré (square) for R1, Ellipse for R5, Pyramid for R6; the regional air operations commanders used ecclesiastical or nobility titles (Baron for R5); the parachuted officers in charge of sabotage training used the names of farming tools (Croc (hook) and Sécateur for R5); the parachuted radio operators drew their names from the Antiquity (Parthe (Parthian) and Ruthène (Ruthenian) for R5).

Left.
A group of résistance fighters equipped with both captured and parachuted weapons (Sten SMGs).
(Collection François de Rochenoise picture)

André Rondenay
a.k.a " André Claude ", " Lemniscate ", " Sapeur ", " Jarry ", " Jean-Louis Lebel " and " Francis Courtois "

Born on 26 August 1913 in Saint-Germain-en-Laye, he was an artillery battery commander on the Maginot line during the Battle of France. Taken prisoner in the Vosges region on 20 June 1940, he was first transferred to a POW cage in Sarrebourg and then in Westphalia in Oflag VIB.

In January 1942, after several escape attempts, André Rondenay was transferred to the famous Colditz fortress, Oflag IV-C, near Lübeck. Undaunted, he managed to escape on 19 December 1942 and to return to France in harrowing conditions. On 25 January 1943, he crossed into Spain but was arrested by the police; thanks to forged ID papers, he managed to escape once again and finally reached London in April 1943.

Volunteering immediately for special duties, André Rondenay was posted to the *Bureau Central de Renseignements et d'Action*. He was trained in intelligence gathering and sabotage operations and as part of mission Lemniscate, was put in charge of the implementation of plan "Tortue" (the Turtle Plan which had been designed to slow down German units and logistics after the Allied landings).

Landed by Lysander in the Tours region on 13 September 1943, he soon reached Paris where he organized a network. In February 1944, Rondenay took the position of André Boulloche who had been arrested on 12 January as the Military Delegate of the Parisian region, which comprised eleven départements. Between February and March 1944, André Rondenay, with a group belonging to the "Patchouli" mission, took part in several raids on factories located in or around Paris. Appointed as Military Delegate of the North zone in April 1944, he received and dispatched his agents all over his area of operations, established liaisons with the PTT (post office) résistance movements in order to prepare for the sabotage of long range underground telephone cables (the Plan Violet) or with the railway service résistance groups in preparation for the implementation of the Plan Vert. After the Normandy landings took place, he joined the maquis of the Aube, Yonne and Nièvre départements. Together with the "Patchouli" mission and the Julien maquis, he took part in several sabotage operations conducted against railways and canal locks.

On 13 June 1944, Colonel Rondenay and members of his group counter-attacked three German companies that had just surrounded some FFI groups in the Lorme region of the Nièvre département, thus allowing the surrounded maquisards to make good their escape. On 27 July 1944, he was arrested by the Germans at the La Muette métro station in Paris. Held at the Fresnes prison, he was about to be deported to Germany on 15 August 1944. Identified by the German security services just before the train left the Pantin station near Paris, he was taken by the Gestapo and driven to Domont, in the Val d'Oise département, at the clairière des quatre chênes (the four oaks clearing) where he was shot.

The American US M1 A1 carbine.
Dropped to résistance movements in very small quantities, it was considered a prestige weapon and highly sought after by officers. It was used indifferently by agents coming from London, Jedburgh or training teams in the maquis. This particular weapon is the folding stock version designed for airborne units.
(Frédéric Vernon collection picture)

Valentin Abeille
a.k.a " Méridien ", " Colleone " and " Fantassin "

Valentin Abeille was born on 8 August 1907 in Alençon. A reserve officer who had been through the Saumur cavalry school, he refused, when the war broke out, to be given a cushy position away from the fight. Instead, he was posted to the 29e Régiment de Dragons and fought in Belgium and France, earning a Croix de Guerre and three citations.

At the end of 1941, he established contact with the Combat résistance movement in Marseille and met its leader Henri Frenay in January 1942. Between May and July 1942, he was involved in the production of clandestine press with other members of Combat. On a recommendation from Marcel Pecq, the regional Combat leader, Valentin Abeille was appointed as départemental leader of Combat for the Jura. Under the alias of "Colleone", he also became the départemental leader of the *Armée Secrète* (AS) for the Jura. In January 1943, hunted down by the Gestapo and with several of his family members under arrest, he joined a maquis in the Jura département before reaching London, during the night of 19 to 20 May 1943 via a pick-up from the clandestine "Orion" landing site located near Cosges.

While in the United Kingdom, Valentin Abeille was posted to the BCRA. Appointed as Military Delegate of Region M (Normandy, Brittany and Anjou), he went through rigorous training before returning, with other Military Delegates and under the alias of "Fantassin", to France during the night of 12 to 13 September 1943 via an air operation near which landed him near the city of Tours.

In only a few months and with the help of his deputy Maurice Guillaudot, he managed to regroup the résistance military forces of the 14 départements of the regions placed under his authority.

Under the alias of "Méridien", he implemented the different plans that had been devised between London and the Résistance (plans Bleu, Violet, Vert). A price was put on his head. Caught in a trap, he was arrested by the Gestapo in Paris on 31 May 1944. Shot and very severely wounded, he was nevertheless brutally interrogated in the Gestapo building of rue des Saussaies. Transferred to the Hôpital de la Pitié, Valentin Abeille died 48 hours later on 2 June 1944 without having spoken a word.

(Musée de l'Ordre de la Libération pictures)

planned sabotage operations were carried out and the maquis, reinforced by new volunteers, went on the offensive.

DENYING MOBILITY TO GERMAN FORCES

Three areas of operations were drawn: a Northern Zone focused on sabotage to halt German reinforcements to Normandy; a South-West/Center area in which the FFI were to conduct offensive actions against the German forces and finally a South/South-East area which was to conduct harasment and interdiction operations along a South-North axis in order to support the landing in Provence (Operation

Top.
After a daring sabotage operation in the Côte d'Or département during the Spring of 1944, a train is blocked on a bridge. The implementation of the Plan Vert initiated by the BCRA led to significant delays in German movements all over France.
(Archives de la SNCF picture)

Left.
A series of BCRA documents; after action reports on sabotage operations in France, operation orders of FFI actions carried out in support of Allied operations and presentation of different armed groups in France before the Normandy landings of June 1944. Bottom right, notice the Plan Vert, which had been produced by the BCRAL.
(Henri-Louis Lévèque collection)

Anvil then renamed Operation Dragoon) which took place on 15 August 1944.

The Normandy and Provence landings were preceded by strategic deception operations. The Fortitude North Plan (or plan Graffham), launched in February 1944, aimed at leading the Germans to believe that the Allied planned operations against Scandinavia, and the Fortitude South, also launched in February 1944, aimed at convincing the Supreme Command of the German forces Oberkommando der Wehrmacht (OKW) that the Normandy landing was only a preliminary operation to a much bigger undertaking planned in the Pas-de-Calais, while at the same time exaggerating the potential of the Allied invasion [18].

Feldmarschall Erwin Rommel, who was then commander of the Army Group B (37 German divisions stationed in France between the mouth of the Escaud and Loire rivers including the 15 divisions of the Seventh Army based in Normandy and Brittany), was one of the rare German commanders to be convinced that the Allied attack would be launched on Normandy. In June 1944, Nazi Germany had 59 divisions spread between France, Belgium and Holland, of which 18 were located south of the Loire. When the Normandy invasion was launched on 6 June 1944, at the end of this first historic day, the OKW was convinced that the Allies had 70 to 72 divisions, while in reality they only fielded 44 divisions. This miscalculation was made possible by the intoxication led by two double agents, Czerniawski (a.k.a "Brutus") and Juan Pujol (a.k.a "Garbo") who operated from 1942 on, under the control of the MI5 Double Cross committee. The Fortitude South plan also aimed at preventing the Fifteenth Army, (made up of 22 divisions including 17 Infantry divisions located between the mouth of the river Seine, the Channel coast, the Pas-de-Calais, the mouth of the Escaut river and Belgium), from reinforcing the Seventh Army which was then engaged in direct combat against the Allied troops in Normandy. The Fortitude South program and the actions of the domestic resistance movements, delayed the arrival of five German divisions, namely the 1st SS Panzer Division (ten day delay), the 116th Panzer Division (six weeks delay), and finally the 84th, 85th and 331st Infantry Divisions (almost two months delay). Those units represented a total of about 70,000 men who were not able to reach the Normandy front in time to achieve the required effect [19].

Top.
In London, the Commissaire à l'information (information commissary) Jacques Soustelle was considered as one of the most faithful collaborators of General de Gaulle. On 27 November 1943, he was appointed as head of the Direction Générale des Services Spéciaux (DGSS), a structure, which was created in October 1943 after the amalgamation of the BCRA and the Algiers-based special services, placed under the authority of General Henri Giraud.
(ECPAD picture)

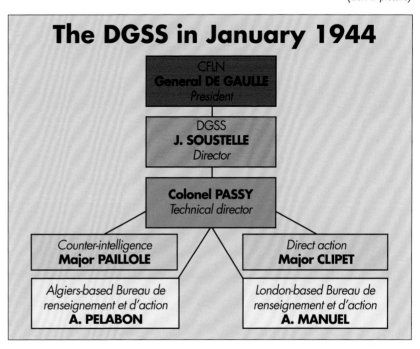

The DGSS in January 1944

CFLN General DE GAULLE President
DGSS J. SOUSTELLE Director
Colonel PASSY Technical director

Counter-intelligence Major PAILLOLE	Direct action Major CLIPET
Algiers-based Bureau de renseignement et d'action A. PELABON	London-based Bureau de renseignement et d'action A. MANUEL

18. On this topic, see Gilbert Bloch, " Les opérations d'intoxication liées aux débarquements de 1944 ", pp. 187-214, in Fabienne Mercier-Bernadet (dir.), *1939-1945 ; La guerre des intelligences.* Paris, éditions Lavauzelle, Collection " Renseignements et guerre secrète ", 2002, 381 pages.

While most missions were successful, some actions result in the arrest of agents, their deportation after torture, and execution. It also happened that some missions were cancelled under pressure from alliance partners. In July 1944, the Caïman Plan, which planned the parachuting of General Billotte and force C agents for mid-August, in the Massif Central, was finally cancelled under pressure from the U.S. services.

The activation of the planned operations was optimal at the time of the Allied landing in Normandy (Operation Overlord) on 6 June 1944. Thus, on the night of 5 to 6 June, following a decision of General Eisenhower, the operations relayed by the DMR, were launched on a large scale.

Already in April, the Résistance had recorded good results, although the epilogue could sometimes be tragic, as, for example, the destruction of one of the largest ammunition depots in France, located in the Hurtebise quarries near Jonzac in Charente-Maritime. The operation was conducted by nineteen-year-old Pierre Ruibet and Claude Gatineau. After two unsuccessful attempts, the explosion killed Pierre Ruibet. Gatineau chose to give himself in order to avoid the execution of 50 hostages in Jonzac. He was shot on 1 July 1944.

Among the operational results of the BCRA, the most immediate was that seven out of the twelve German divisions that had been earmarked for that mission were unable to leave for Normandy to block the Allies progression from their Normandy bridgeheads before

19. Gilbert Bloch, *op. cit.,* page 211.

Top.
In front of the 7th arrondissement townhall in Paris on 26 October 1944: Left to right: Lieutenant Christian Longetti MBE, officer in charge of direct Action for the RD-BOA who then took part in the SAARF mission, Captain Puech Samson DSO from the Free French 2 SAS and Major Michel Pichard, military delegate of Région P3.
(Famille Longetti picture)

Left.
Differents insignias and badges worn by Christian Longetti MBE. Left to right and top to bottom; British Parachute Regiment beret badge with the crown cut off as per Free French fashion; "France" shoulder title; British para wings with navy blue backing as worn on the Free French Air Force walking out uniform; british-made Free French para wings; in the center, french-made bullion Free French para wings; British para wings with green backing as worn on the battle dress; on the left a picture of Christian Longetti taken at the end of 1944; the SAARF mission sleeve badge (a winged arrow breaking a chain); some ribbons; a variant of the SAARF shoulder title, (all the SAARF badges are british-made), and Jedburghs.
(Longetti family collection)

S.A.A.R.F.

Christian Longetti
a.k.a "Esch"

Christian Longetti was born on 28 December 1920. As early as 1940, he took part in the organisation of a rat line in the bassin de Briey (Meurthe-et-Moselle département) in order to help escaping French POWs to cross the Luxembourg borders in to reach the non-occupied zone.

Arrested by the Gestapo in May 1942 in Arbois, he escaped in the Belfort train station during his transfer and managed to reach the non-occupied zone. Two months latter, he joined the OCM intelligence service for the non-occupied zone and performed several missions as a liaison agent between Paris and Lyon. In March 1943, he joined the *Bureau des Opérations Aériennes* (Air Operations Bureau) of the East region. In May 1943, he became a BCRA agent under the alias of "Chantre" and helped to organise over 200 parachute and pick-up operations in the Nièvre, Côte d'Or, Haute-Saône, Jura and Saône-et-Loire départements. He also organised some sabotage operations and was tasked with the allotment of parachute delivered weapons to the different résistance movements. Wounded to the leg during a joint operation with the Chatillon *maquis*, tracked by the Gestapo, his return to London had to be aborted when his Lysander was shot down. Promoted to the rank of Lieutenant and operations officer of the C1 Region from June 1944, he organised, with the Mourmelon *maquis,* a series of guerrilla operations in the Reims region. He also took part in the clearing of the last German units in the Marne département.

From 1 October 1944, Christian Longetti was placed under DGER command. On 23 December 1944, he was sent to London and posted to the *Détachement de Liaison des Services Spéciaux* (Special Services Liaison Detachment) with the alias of " Esch". In March 1945, he was posted to the Special Allied Airborne Reconnaissance Force (SAARF) as a Second Lieutenant. He was parachuted in Germany on 6 May 1945 in order to carry out sabotage operations and was wounded by a land mine on 1 June 1945.

Top right.
After a stay in a British hospital after having been wounded in the Hamburg region in May 1945, Christian Longetti was sent for convalescence at the Puy en Velay in the Haute Loire département.
(Longetti family collection)

Left and Bottom.
Christian Longetti's Fairbairn-Sykes commando dagger and compass.

Bottom and right.
Several French ID documents, both genuine and forged (with the false identity of Christian Ladler), as well as some membership cards of British clubs.
(Longetti family collection)

Top.
An american-made " Ike " Battle Dress dated 1946 which belonged to Christian Longetti. The different insignias and badges are: Captain's rank, French-made Free French para wings, British-made "mosquito" Free French badge and the ribbons of the Légion d'Honneur, Croix de Guerre, médaille de la Résistance, MBE (Military division) and médaille de la France libre.

Assessment of sabotage actions

According to reports drafted in late 1944, nearly 2,000 high voltage poles had been destroyed by the Résistance resulting in numerous power cuts. Interruptions of electricity supplies were far from negligible.

Over a 320 days period in 1944, the 220,000-volt lines passing through the Alps and the Massif Central and supplying Paris were only fully operational for 63 days.

Within 24 hours of the Normandy landing, the British secret services had registered 486 railway cuttings. Out of the 1,050 railways interruptions programmed in the Green plan, 950 were carried out as well as 180 derailments of trains or locomotives.

Previously, the destruction of locomotives had also been one of the RAF's tasks. From December 1943, the sabotage of locomotives in marshalling yards was favoured: 137 were destroyed in December 1943, 322 in January 1944 and 198 in February 1944.

During the summer of 1944, the Résistance carried out the destruction of 270 railway bridges and 1,750 locomotives and conducted 4,440 railways cuttings. In comparison, the results of road interdiction operations were not as impressive.

Air operations sometimes compensated for the failures of sabotage missions. In November 1943, for example, three BCRA agents, Marcel Suarès, Pierre Brioux and François Fouquat intended to sabotage a ball bearing plant in the Lyon area (mission Patchouli).

As they could not get the required explosives in a timely manner, the RAF bombed the site instead. However, the Suarès team managed to successfully complete other sabotage missions.

Bottom.
The impressive results of railway sabotage in the Spring of 1944.
(Photo Archives SNCF)

12 June 1944. The destruction and delaying actions plans carried out by the internal resistance also compensated for the temporary halt of the flow of allied reinforcements caused by the sea storm on 7 and 8 June 1944.

During that period, from July to September 1944, nearly 50,000 containers were dropped against only about 3,000 in 1943. Each container could hold 150 kg of equipment.

According to Passy, the operational results of the offensive actions of the Résistance convinced Eisenhower to increase the Allied support to the French irregulars. So in July 1944, he ordered large quantities of weapons to be airdroped in maquis-held areas. Still, a certain amount of distrust remained on the reliability of the different movements as evidenced by the low number of heavy weapons such as mortars supplied to the Résistance: 47 in August 1944, and 123 in September 1944.

But the lack of weapons and the difficulty in organizing parachute drops also contributed to the demise of some maquis, such as the Vercors maquis which was anihilated in July 1944 by German glider and mountain troops: 4,000 members of the resistance, half of them unarmed, were surrounded by nearly 10,000 German soldiers and Vichy security forces elements. 600 résistance fighters and civilians were killed as well as about one hundred German soldiers.

The joint action of the Jedburgh, Sussex and Proust teams

Starting in the Spring of 1944, in Great-Britain, the FFL formed teams dedicated to special operations behind German lines in occupied France. These teams were composed of Allied agents: a mission head, a radio operator and a Canadian, American or English assistant. 13 such teams were parachuted into France in June 1944 with orders to liaise with the maquis and to provide them with weapons and equipment and to mentor them into actions. These actions were to be led according to the orders and plan of the Allied High Command while maintaining a radio contact with the BCRA. In May 1944, only 10,000 resistant were considered as well equipped and trained while another 85,000 others, even though they had weapons, were considered as in need of some serious training.

Between June and September 1944, the 8th Air Force's B-17 provided the bulk of weapons and equipment airdrops in order to equip some 350,000 résistance fighters.

In conjunction with the Jedburgh, nearly sixty Sussex plans teams were dropped from Brittany to the Belgian border (see boxed text). Their intelligence gathering missions involved being parachuted directly on the rear of the enemy, in a corridor established between 60 and 100 km from the coast, in order to collect as much intelligence about the enemy forces and dispositions, location, movement, etc as possible... Those teams had to follow the movements of the German troops by showing examplary mobility and discretion.

At the end of the war, elements of the Jedburgh, Sussex and Proust teams were tasked to work in the 19 centres where deportees and prisoners of war from France and Germany were screened and subjected to counterintelligence measures.

In the end, 25% of the guerrilla operations were carried out in support of Overlord and 50% in support of the landing in Provence. Finally, nearly 25% were devoted to destabilizing and harassment actions against retreating German forces.

Center.
Pennant of an FFI group from the Var département.
(Collection AERI)

Right.
From July 1944 on, tens of thousands of maquisards armed, trained and led by BCRA, OSS and SOE teams fought German military and para military forces in several areas of occupied France. They did not always achieve their objectives but the pressure this " army of the interior " put on the enemy was real and from August 1944 on, the maquisards managed to free entire départements without outside help.
(25ᵉ DIM picture)

Over 560 Agents Deployed on Missions

No less than 129 BCRA members, including Passy[1], became Companions de la Libération, the highest award a Free French could receive. Twelve of them died on operation after having swallowed their cyanide pill in order to escape capture and torture. Covert actions by both air and sea facilitated the transit of over 560 agents between England and France on behalf of the BCRA. In comparison, F and RF sections of the SOE each sent to France nearly 450 agents. Between 1940 and 1944, the various services sent nearly 1,500 covert agents to France[2].

Even though his leadership was not accepted by all, Charles de Gaulle managed to gather around him vastly different men who all shared a common goal, to free France, a common enemy, Nazi Germany, and a strong taste for action. In spite of sometimes diverging interests, the French and the British always managed to place the common struggle first.

With the end of Second World War, a new period opened for the secret agents of Charles de Gaulle. Most of the BCRA members returned to Paris at the end of September 1944 to be integrated into the General of Directorate Special Services (DGSS).

General de Gaulle changed the habits of the counter intelligence services (CE) putting an end to the military primacy in this area which had prevailed in France since the First World War. The DGSS was disbanded on 23 October 1944 and replaced on 26 October by the General Directorate of Studies

Top.
On 5 September 1944, in the liberated city of Chalon-sur-Saône, André Jarrot (in the center, wearing a beret) reviews different maquisard groups that took part in the liberation of the region. At this date, this BCRA character had already been parachuted on four different occasions in occupied France! After having been parachuted on 9 July 1944, he obtained, thanks to a pick-up operation going to London, a resupply drop of weapons and equipment which " followed through " on 10 August 1944 in Sennecey-le-Grand.
(Maison de la Résistance et de la Libération du Chalonais picture)

and Research (*Direction Générale des Études et de la Recherche* -DGER) which comprized a large proportion of civilians with an FFI background. The DGER was under the authority of the head of government and, as a logical consequence of this restructuring of the secret services, counter-intelligence and military security became two separate structures, again based on General de Gaulle's decision (despite the efforts of Paul Paillole to prevent such a situation). A meeting of the National Defence Council on 17 November 1944 decided that the former Directorate of Military Security (Direction de Sécurité militaire - DSM) was to be divided and reorganized between the DGER and a military security section falling under the chief of the general staff. Paillole refused to take command of this organization and resigned, partly because he was not satisfied with the background checks and credentials of the DGER agents.

Jacques Soustelle was designated as the head of the DGER, replacing Paillole.

In the following months, the special services were expanded.

On 30 January 1946, the military security section was transformed into a genuine military security service, headed by Colonel Labadie. A few months later, on 16 November 1946, the Direction de la Surveillance du Territoire (Directorate of Territorial Surveillance or DST) was created and placed under the orders of Roger Wybot

As for the DGER, it was transformed, by a decision taken during a cabinet meeting dated 28 December 1945, into the *Service de Documentation Extérieure et de Contre-Espionnage* (Service of External Documentation and Counterintelligence or SDECE). From January 1946, Passy was appointed director of this new service, with Daniel Cordier as his Chief of Staff. On 15 January, the SDECE was attached to the Prime Minister, only a few days before the resignation of Charles de Gaulle as President of the Republic, and a few weeks before Passy's resignation. Henri Ribière replaced him at the head of the SDECE. A new page in the history of the French shadow fighters was about to begin: the Secret Services of the Fourth Republic...

1. As many others, Passy was made a Compagnon de la Libération during the Spring of 1943.
2. Jean-Louis Crémieux-Brilhac, *La France libre. De l'appel du 18 juin à la Libération*. Paris, éditions Gallimard, 1996, page 744.

Top.
In the courtyard of the French embassy in London on 14 June 1944 during a Croix de la Libération award ceremony to four BCRA agents. In the center, wearing a beret, the very discreet André Manuel. Passy's deputy was nevertheless considered as one of the BCRA founding fathers.
(ECPAD picture)

In the courtyard of the French embassy in London on 14 June 1944 during a Croix de la Libération award ceremony. Left to right: Major "Mary" Basset DSO, MC (a saboteur during the Armada mission), Michel Pichard MBE (BOA national coordinator), André Jarrot DCM, MM and Pierre Guilhemon (another saboteur during the Armada mission). *(ECPAD picture)*

INDEX OF PROPES NAMES

On 15 June 1957, during the inauguration of a commemorative plaque at 1 Dorset Square. Maurice Bourgès-Maunoury DSO, André Jarrot DCM, MM, "Mary" Basset DSO, MC, Pierre Deshayes DSO, Jean Rosenthal MC and Pierre Guilhemon can be identified.
(Musée de l'ordre de la Libération picture)

GLOSSARY

A/M: Military action section of the BCRA
BAM: Anti national activities bureau
BCRA: Central bureau of intelligence and action
BCRAM: Central bureau of intelligence and military action
BIP: Press and information bureau
BO: Operational block
BRAA: Algiers-based intelligence and action bureau
BRAL: London-based intelligence and action bureau
CAF: Committee for action in France
CDLL: Those of the Liberation
CDLR: Those of the Résistance
CE: Counter intelligence section of the BCRA
CESM: Counter intelligence and military security service
CFLN: French national liberation committee
CGE: General study committee
CNI: Interior national commissary
CNR: National Résistance Council
COI: Coordinator of Intelligence Gathering
COMAC: Résistance military action committee
Comidac: Action in France committee
COSSAC: Chief of Staff to the Supreme Allied Commander
CCZN: North zone coordination committee
CCZS: South zone coordination committee
DBLE: 13th half-brigade of the Foreign Legion
DGER: General directorate of studies and researches
DGSS: Algiers-based general directorate of special services
DMR: Regional military delegates
DSR-RM: Directorate of intelligence services and military security
DST: Directorate of the surveillance of the territory
DTSS: Technical directorate of special services

DZ: Drop Zone
EM: Staff
EMFFI: Staff of the French forces of the interior
EMFILA: Staff of the interior forces and of administrative liaison
FFC: Fighting French Forces
FFI: French forces of the Interior
FFL: Free French Forces
FTPF: Communist résistance movements
IGAME: General inspector of the administration in extraordinary mission
IS: Intelligence Service
MI6: Military Intelligence
MMLA: Military mission of administrative liaison
M/N: Non-military section of the BCRA
ORA: Armed résistance organisation
OSS: Office of Strategic Service
OVRA: Italian Fascist political police
OKW: German armed forces supreme command
R: Intelligence section of the BCRA
RF: British liaison section between SOE and BCRA
RAF: Royal Air Force
SDECE: Overseas documentation and counter-intelligence service
SFIO: French Socialist Party
SHAEF: Supreme Headquarters Allied Expeditionnary Forces
SFHQ: Special Forces Headquarters
SOAM: Air and maritime operations service
SOE: Special Operations Executive.
STO: Mandatory work duty
SR: Intelligence service
ZNO: Non occupied zone

Symbol of the French Resistance. Action team emplacing
a demolition charge on a railway.
(Archive SNCF)

BIBLIOGRAPHY

BOOKS

- Amicale des réseaux action de la France combattante, *Les réseaux Actions de la France combattante*. Paris, editions France Empire, 1986, 296 pages.
- Sébastien Albertelli, *Les Services secrets du général de Gaulle. Le BCRA 1940-1944*. Paris, editions Perrin, 2010, 617 pages.
- Jean-Louis Crémieux-Brilhac, *La France libre. De l'appel du 18 juin à la Libération*. Paris, editions Gallimard, 1996, 969 pages.
- Guy Perrier, *Le colonel Passy et les services secrets de la France libre*. Paris, editions Hachette Littératures, 1999, 308 pages.
- Colonel Passy, *Mémoires du chef des services secrets de la France libre*. Paris, editions Odile Jacob, 2000, 816 pages.
- Edgard Tupët-Thomé, *Special Air Service. 1940-1945. L'épopée d'un parachutiste en France occupée*. Paris, editions Grasset, 1981, 250 pages.

SPECIFIC STUDIES

- Alya Aglan, *Le réseau Jade-Fitzroy: de l'intelligence service au BCRA. Etudes sur l'Histoire du renseignement*. Paris, editions Lavauzelle, 1998, 280 pages.
- Robert Belot, Gilbert Karpman, *La circulation du renseignement clandestin dans la résistance: enjeux politiques et techniques de la cryptographie. La guerre des intelligences*. Paris, editions Lavauzelle, Collection "Renseignements et guerre secrète", 2002, 381 pages.
- Gilbert Bloch, *Les opérations d'intoxication liées aux débarquements de 1944. La guerre des intelligences*. Paris, editions Lavauzelle, Collection "Renseignements et guerre secrète", 2002, 381 pages.
- Marie-Thérèse Chabord, *Le bureau central de renseignements et d'action de la France libre. Structures et évolution (1940-1944)*.
- Collectif, " Aviateurs et Résistants " in Revue *Icare*, volumes 1 to 5 (n°141, 144, 148, 151 et 153).
- Philippe Egu, *Recherches sur la notion de réseau de renseignement dans la Résistance. Etudes sur l'Histoire du renseignement*. Paris, editions Lavauzelle, 1998, 280 pages.
- Serge Larcher, " Le Plan Sussex " in *Symboles et Traditions* n°176 (october 1990), and " Le Plan Proust " in *Symboles et Traditions* n°185 (january-march 2003).
- Sébastien Laurent, *Les services spéciaux de la France Libre: politique et légitimité républicaine. L'exploitation du renseignement en Europe et aux Etats-Unis des années 1930 aux années 1960*. Paris, editions Economica, 2001.
- Jean-Louis Perquin, *Parachutages et atterrissages clandestins*, et *Les opérateurs radio clandestins*. Paris, editions Histoire et Collections, collection "Résistance".
- Guillaume Piketty, "La mission Arquebuse-Brumaire" in *Espoir* n°135.
- Bertrand Souquet, "Les Jedburgh " in *Symboles et Traditions*, n° 191.
- Bertrand Warusfel, *Histoire de l'organisation du contre-espionnage française entre 1871 et 1945. Etudes sur l'Histoire du renseignement*. Editions Lavauzelle, 1998, 280 pages.

SOURCES

- Fonds d'archives 3AG2 (1 à 605), Archives Nationales (Paris)
- Livre blanc du BCRA (redaction by Monsieur and Madame Heissel, M. Guillet and Daniel Cordier). Nationales Archives (Paris).

ACKNOWLEDGEMENT

The author wants to express his sincere gratitude to the following people: Jean-Louis Perquin and Eric Micheletti for their support as well as Bertrand Souquet, Rémy Longetti, Bernard de la Tousche, Olivier Pigoreau, François de Rochenoire, Jean-Louis Le Bihon, Jean-Thomas Duclos, Frédéric Vernon, Henri-Louis Lévèque who opened up their collections as well as Nathalie Genet-Rouffiac, Joachim Pol and Dominique Soulier who runs the Musée du Plan Sussex.

IN THE SAME COLLECTION

LES OPÉRATEURS RADIO CLANDESTINS
ISBN: 978-2-35250-182-4

THE CLANDESTINE RADIO OPERATORS
ISBN: 978-2-35250-183-1

LES PARACHUTAGES ET ATTERRISSAGES CLANDESTINS - TOME I
ISBN: 978-2-35250-248-7

CLANDESTINE PARACHUTE AND PICK-UP OPERATIONS - VOLUME I
ISBN: 978-2-35250-249-4

COMING SOON

THE SUSSEX PLAN, by Dominique Soulier
CLANDESTINE PARACHUTE AND PICK-UP OPERATIONS volume 2, by Jean-Louis Perquin

THIS BOOK WAS EDITED BY ERIC MICHELETTI.
DESIGN AND LAYOUT MATTHIEU PLEISSINGER. TRANSLATED BY VALERIE CAPO.

Histoire & Collections

SA au capital de 182938,82

5, avenue de la République
F-75541 Paris Cédex 11 – FRANCE
Tel: +33(0)1 40 21 18 20 / Fax: +33(0)1 47 00 51 11
www.histoireetcollections.com

This book has been designed, typed, laid-out and processed by *Histoire & Collections* on fully integrated computer equipment.
Color separation: Studio H&C.
Print by Calidad Grafica, Spain, European Union,
March 2013.